ok online at www.trafford.com
rs@trafford.com

l titles are also available at major online book retailers.

United States of America.

269-7423-6 (sc)
269-7484-7 (e)

08/27/2011

 www.trafford.com

:a & international
8 232 4444 (USA & Canada)
83 6864 ♦ fax: 812 355 4082

MARIS

and

Other Scrib

Lucile McCarty

Order this b
or email ord

Most Traffo

© Copyrigh
All rights res
system, or tra
recording, or

Printed in th

ISBN: 978-1
ISBN: 978-1

Trafford re

North Ame
toll-free: 1 8
phone: 250

MARISA

Marisa had been an angelette since she was ten. She knew she had come to Heaven a long time ago. In Heaven one never counted the years, for God the Father was there. One could praise Him days on end and never be tired. Too, He taught one about such interesting tasks.   Well, He taught one when that one would take instruction. Marisa was one of those angelettes who had spells. "Balky spells" the Archangel Michael called them.

Marisa was artistic. As an artistic angelette, she had been elated to be assigned to paint the animals that were being born on earth. Now, God could just have willed each animal's color and marking. Instead, to give the angelettes a part in helping Mankind on earth, He had decided long ago to set up interesting tasks for them. He knew ten year olds become bored quite quickly.

God assigned Marisa the task of painting cows, her favorite animal on earth. She liked all kinds of calves back then, and here in the paint group they painted calves of all kinds.

Now, Marisa had problems with her task. It wasn't that she painted poorly. It wasn't that her ideas were bad. It wasn't that she insisted on painting every calf the same. Marisa just wouldn't paint the calves the right colors on her own babies nor would she leave the other angelettes' babies alone. When they painted the Hereford calves, certain rules had to be followed. The calves had to be rich red with white on their faces and a bit of white on their tummies. They could have white socks: one, two, three, or even four. Certainly, any angelette could vary the area of white, but there was no chance to use dabs of gold around the horns-to-be or touches of blue over the eyes. In fact, all their eyes had to be brown. Many a time Michael had set Marisa in the corner to contemplate exactly what a Hereford should look like.

Then there were the Angus, both red and black. Little room for innovation in painting them existed. They were harder than the Herefords for Marisa to paint. Any angelette--even one without artistic talent--could paint an all black or red calf with one white blotch on the underside just behind the belly button. A dab or two of pink on the black ones or an artistic "S" of white down the back of a red one livened up its appearance--at least in Marisa's eyes.

Michael tried many times to get Marisa to see the sense in keeping each calf painted to resemble its mother and father. His instruction, however, just went right by Marisa, who was off in her paint world. He determined to talk to God about the situation. He was at his wits' end with her.

One day he made an appointment with God just to talk specifically about his problem with Marisa. After God gave him the perfect solution, Michael could have kicked himself for waiting so long to talk with Him. Marisa was to be placed at the edge of the group of painter angelettes and given only two colors: black and white. She was to be promoted to be the only painter of Holstein calves. She would be able to make all kinds of designs on them so her creativity would not be squashed. Only her choice of colors would be limited.

With fear and trembling, Marisa answered when Michael called her name to come to the front of the studio the next day. "Marisa," he announced to the group, "Marisa is being promoted to be the sole painter of Holstein babies. She will have her easel set over by the northernmost window of Heaven so she can see all the momma and papa Holsteins in the world. If she wants to paint a calf like either one of them or combine them she can. If she wants to create a new pattern on the coat of a calf, she can. Her creativeness will be limited only by her imagination." He didn't mention that she would have only two colors of paint, but Marisa realized that when she moved her easel to that northernmost window and looked down at all the momma and poppa Holsteins. But as it is in heaven, Marisa immediately saw the good task that God had set her to. She would be able to paint all the kinds of designs.

Immediately, she put up her paper and readied her colors. Even though she had only two colors to work in, she went to the brush bin to select one hundred brushes. She picked out thin ones, medium ones, wider ones, and wide-wide-wide ones. She certainly would need that many kinds to do all the various designs that were popping into her head.

As she painted her first heifer baby that was to be born soon, she decided to put a daisy on its forehead with a matching one on its belly. The second one had almost a scallop of white around its nose. And the third had an all white body except for black ears and a black tail. As the baby calves were born on earth, each was different from all rest. Its momma thought her baby was the most beautiful of all the babies.

In the months that passed, Marisa painted many, many Holstein babies. Michael's task of supervising the painting angelettes was much easier. The other angelettes knew their babies would be the right colors. And Marisa could be as creative as she wished. In fact, she'll be painting Holstein babies for years to come, for she has so many designs in mind.

JULIUS

50 A. D.

I awoke, the blinding sunlight hitting my eyes. Something on the bed moved. I turned to see a slight, dark-haired Jewess lying there, still asleep. As she stirred I recalled the night before.

Several of us had gone out to the "local gathering place." Since we Roman soldiers were so far from home, we often frequented these gathering places. None of us planned to marry and settle down in this part of the world. We planned to serve out this occupation time and go back to Rome or Florence to our families and apprenticeships in the business world of our fathers. We'd find a statuesque Greek or fiery Roman girl to marry, certainly no Jewess.

Here, we were the occupiers so we could have what we wanted. This girl lying here was one I had forced to come to my quarters. She had said she was hurrying to a sick aunt but I hadn't believe it. Any girl out that time of night had to be looking for quick money by using her body.

She woke, startled by seeing me. Fear crept into her face. "I'm not going to harm you," I said. "Here's your fee." She shook her head and tugged at the bed covers. "You can go. I'm getting up. Need to report to my command." She cowered there while I dressed. Feeling disgusted with myself and my having forced her to sleep with me, I turned my back to her, pulled on my sandals and caught up my sword. Hopefully, I had covered my disgust. I playfully tapped my sword point on her and said, "Be gone, my beauty. And don't tempt me again."

As centurion, he was the leader of a hundred men. He was an example of a fit, handsome soldier. As he walked toward his headquarters, the Jewish children scurried out of his way. They'd turn to gawk at the rattle of his sword. Mothers tucked little ones behind them. Actually, there was no need for them to fear Julius. When he was not drinking, he was kind, even gentle. He wanted to pat the little tykes on the head as he did his nephews and nieces. He had even learned basic Aramaic so he could talk with this captured people.

That evening when he returned to his quarters, the money he had tossed to the Jewess lay on the table. He rammed it into his money bag. Why had she not taken her fee? Maybe she had been going to her sick aunt's. Oh, well, it was over and done with. Her loss was his gain. Falling across the bed, he dropped off to sleep. He dreamed of home and the blue, blue Mediterranean, which bordered his old hometown, the little town where his family had lived before his father had taken a high place in Caesar's government.

A rap on the makeshift door awakened him. It was only his landlady calling him to the evening meal. He was not overly fond of Jewish cooking; but he got up, splashed tepid water from the basin in his eyes, and went to the kitchen.

The brown eyes of her two young boys peered at him over a low windowsill. Though he would have enjoyed talking with the boys, he never attempted to. He presumed their mother had told them to stay out of the foreigner's way. The Romans had killed her husband when they quelled one of the many Jewish riots. He knew she disliked having to take him as a boarder. What he paid her was so much more than she could make as a winnower.

As he finished the soup, a clatter came from without the window. The two boys had turned and he heard, "Halloo, boys. Is Julius here?" Pushing his chair back Julius strode to the door. A dust covered Clodius met him. "You are to report tomorrow by six. You're going home!"

Home! His recent dream was coming true. Home! His thoughts quickly turned to "Why? What had happened? Or was to happen?"

Clodius seemed to read his mind. "There's a Roman citizen who has been imprisoned. He has appealed to Caesar. Festus is sending him as soon as arrangements can be made. You have been picked to see him safely there. He is a man of the movement called The Way. When he was arrested, no one knew he was a Roman citizen. He is both a Jew and a Roman citizen. What about that!"

Julius had heard about a trial going on for a Jew who claimed to be a Roman citizen. This Jew, said to be a man of The Way—whatever that was—reportedly was able to confound Felix, the former governor. In fact, Felix had gone back to Rome without settling the case. Ah! The man was still a prisoner in Herod's place. He had supposed him to be dead by now. How lucky that he himself was a part of the Augustan cohort so he was never assigned to guard duty at a prison. How lucky Festus learned that the man was a Roman citizen. Killing or even imprisoning a Roman citizen as one would a Jew would have brought King Claudius' ire down upon him. Felix could catch it, too.

Turning, he called to the landlady. Though he knew she had overheard Clodius' announcement, he repeated it for her. He would be paying his rent and board to date as soon as he knew the departure date.

The morning after reporting to his chief, he went to secure passage for himself, his three soldiers, the prisoner named Paul and the Jewish doctor, Luke by name, who thought he should accompany the prisoner. It seemed the prisoner had developed joint pains from the cold and dampness in the prison. The group would have to travel to Adramyttium to board the ship. The captain set the sailing time as three o'clock two days later.

Julius charged a deputy to secure two cloaks of Sicilian goat hair for the journey. Since the prisoner was a Roman citizen, he would keep him warm. Before the deputy could leave, Julius changed the order to three cloaks. The Jewish doctor might as well have one. He might be invaluable on the trip should anyone become ill.

That day, Antonius, the head of the military detachment, sent Julius word the prisoner had asked that another man name Aristarchus be allowed to go along. Since Aristarchus didn't have any charges against him, Antonius had approved his going. Paul would be in chains; the others would be carrying the small amount of baggage they and Paul have.

Julius was prepared for taking charge of the prisoner when the entourage arrived from the prison palace. He had gathered his few belongings and paid his room and board by mid-morning. Observing the prisoner he noted that this man was small. Why was he so feared by the governor? He did have the look of a philosopher with his round bald head and bushy brows. It must be the ideas he championed that caused such fear. Since Paul was a Jew, one would have supposed the rest of the Jews would have been upset that he had been imprisoned for over two years. Probably his being a Roman citizen and his at least being off the street caused them to be disinterested for the time being.

The little group--Julius, the prisoner, the doctor, the friends, and the three soldiers who were to accompany them to the ship—set off for Caesarea by foot. The road was dusty. They had nearly emptied the water bottles by the time they arrived. The trip had not been leisurely by any means since so many people met them along the way to wish the prisoner "God speed." Julius did not know what god they were talking about. Several times he had told people to move out of the way. He and his men were alert lest these crowds turn on them in an attempt to free the prisoner.

The port smelled of animals, the sea, the fish, and dust. Swarthy people in loose robes stood about. The sailors themselves had tied up their garments as they loaded the ship. Now, they were herding a few of the animals on board. What a fine sail this would be with the animals! At least the sun had become bright. The golden sea stretched endless west.

The journey would be long, for this coaster called at many little ports along the way. As Julius talked with the captain, he was pleased to learn at least Tyre would not be a stop this trip. He was assured the goats and sheep would be safely quartered at one end of the ship. He might have the task of taking this prisoner to Rome but he certainly didn't intend to sleep among animals on the way. Their bleating and baaing would be enough to endure. Another entourage of six Jewish prisoners and eight soldiers booked on the same coaster appeared. The captain ordered the anchor weighed.

The next day, the port of Sidon was a welcome sight. The captain noted an unusually large group of people gathered at the landing. When the ship docked, Julius found many of them had come to see the prisoner Paul. In fact, Paul, Luke and Aristarchus greeted many of them by name. They had brought some special provisions and clothing for the prisoner. Julius went down the short gangplank to check out the items. Since they seemed to be only helps to make the trip more comfortable, he allowed Paul to go ashore to get them. Paul remained in chains as he chatted with his friends while Luke and Aristarchus mingled among them.

Julius stood close by. He was puzzled by something Paul said: "I will continue to be an ambassador for Christ even though I am in chains." Oh, Julius had heard about this Christ person. All Rome's captured peoples had strange gods to worship, but to be an ambassador? Ambassadors went with kingdoms, not itinerants.

The dock hands quickly unloaded the goods for this point. Julius was glad to see the sheep and goats were being herded off. Several young boys came aboard to clean the area where they had been held. The trip would much quieter now; the air would certainly be more pleasant

Once again on board, the captain ordered the crew to turn the vessel out to open water.

They had to call at Myra, the southern most point of Asia Minor. Since it was autumn, they would be taking a northern route. There would be sufficient wind to push against on the lee side of Cyprus; but at this time of year it was best to take this route. The closer the route out in the Great Sea was just too choppy.

Paul and his companions asked to visit with the other prisoners. Julius could see no harm in allowing such a visit so he unshackled Paul. He accompanied the small group. When they had re-boarded, one of the other prisoners had complained of being seasick. Paul put his hand out to touch him and prayed. The fellow looked up at Paul and studied him as he talked. Julius listened. Paul talked about an experience he had had that changed his life completely. It had happened on a road near Damascus. Julius wondered as he listened as to how one could hear a god speak audibly. He had never heard of such a happening from a sane man. From Paul's story, Julius gathered that this Jesus was the reason Paul was a prisoner. Julius thought, "It's stupid to be an ambassador for someone who, as far as I know, doesn't have a kingdom." The ship began to pitch some. As it rounded the tip of Cyprus, the winds strengthened. Julius thought it best to secure his prisoner so he hustled him back to the shackles. Luke and Aristarchus stayed to talk.

Julius noted that the four of the other guards and one of his soldiers stayed close to listen.

The stop at Myra was even more welcome than the one at Sidon. Julius took the prisoner into a little shop with him to secure a warm meal. Luke and Aristarchus also came in. Four of the other soldier came in to get the food for their prisoners whom they had seated by a small building. Before Paul and his friends ate, they repeated a custom Julius had already seen them perform many times thus far. They bowed their heads and muttered words. The captain came in. He offered to oversee Paul while Julius secured passage on a larger ship bound for Rome.

Only one Alexandrian corn ship stood in the harbor. The captain, an Egyptian, assured Julius that his was the last ship for the season that would be going to Italy. She was loaded with grain but there would be space for the group. The captain was curious as to Julius' taking a ship instead of going over land at this time of year. Julius told him about the prisoner he was escorting. Too, he would chance the water rather than the mountainous passages that might be impassable. He didn't want to spend all winter in a little mountain village with his prisoner and his friends. Though the people who had met them at their two ports of call did not seem to be antagonistic toward him and his soldiers, he had to be aware that these Jews might be a part of a plot to whisk Paul away.

Collecting Paul and the others, Julius led them aboard. As they joined the other passengers Paul commented on the sturdiness of the ship. He asked to walk to the front of the ship. Julius complied. Paul looked at the carving of Isis, the Greek goddess whom the Greeks called the mother of the gods. "Fine carving," he said to Luke, who had followed, "but we know she is not the mother of our God." Luke replied, "It is heartbreaking that even the Romans have become so enamored of Greek philosophy that they hear so little of the gospel when it is preached to them."

As the ship entered the sea, the winds grew fiercer. Often even the crew was ill from the pitching waves. Luke suggested they lie down as much as possible. He administered medicines to those most ill. Sailing was slow. Paul and his friends talked of past times. Paul spoke of Tarsus, the city which was home. He told them about the cold water of Cydus where he had learned to swim. His family had gone to the Taurus Mountains each summer to escape the steamy heat in Tarsus. If they had stayed at home, he would have slept on a raised platform in the courtyard.

After the first week, they were on half way to Cnidus. Aristarchus had decided to leave the party to strike out for his home in Macedonia. As he spoke with Julius about leaving, he indicated he would visit the congregations in Mileta, Ephesus, Troas, and other points to the north. It was apparent to Julius that Aristachus was to carry messages to these congregations from Paul. Aristarchus hoped to catch a small vessel calling at these ports. His leaving made Julius no difference. Just one less person to look out for.

Paul seemed particularly anxious about Aristarchus' going to Ephesus. As Julius idly listened to the friends' talking, he learned Paul had almost lost his life in Ephesus because he had preached that Diana was only an idol. His God was a living God, one who could respond to people, who loved them, who asked only that they believe in Him and He would answer their prayers. Julius reasoned one has to believe in any god to get his prayers answered. No wonder the silversmiths wanted Paul dead. He was ruining their trinket business. Paul had cheated death by being whisked away by friends. "Just what I have to watch for," thought Julius.

Another week passed before they made it to Cnidus. The crew and passengers were grateful for a night's rest as they anchored in the bay. During that week Julius had overheard Paul's telling of his joy in establishing a church in Antioch of Pisidia and the heartache he had suffered when the Jews contradicted him, calling him a blasphemer. He heard of a Roman proconsul Sergius Paulus, who had sent for Paul to tell him about this Jesus character. He enjoyed the story of Paul's being accused of defiling the Jewish temple by taking an uncircumcised gentile in. What an uproar that must have caused! Though Julius took these stories as exaggerations, he did see that some of the crew and soldiers listened wide-eyed.

Aristarchus and Paul rose early the morning they arrived in Cnidus. Again, they bowed their heads together. Julius could hear Paul saying, "And keep him safe, O Lord, as he undertakes this trip." From Aristarchus he heard, "Keep this ship at peace." They would certainly need peace from the sea to make better time than they had been making.

Before they left Cnidus, the Aegean's usual turquoise waters turned leaden. Thunder clouds hung low. The captain lay out his sailing plans to Julius. "We will try to cross the Aegean here, go right below Achaia, move up the coast of Macedonia, and cross the Adriatic to Italy. We can sail up the coast of Italy or to the south, hugging the coastline, and then north to Rhegium. We know all sea lanes are safe. The Romans keep them so." Julius agreed, mostly because he was at the mercy of the captain's expertise.

They had been out to sea a half day when the winds became fiercer. No matter how they tried, the crew could not get back to the planned course. The captain, having made the trip many times, knew they were headed for Crete. There was no turning back, for they would be bucking the wind. Again, many of the crew fell ill. Miraculously the prisoner seemed to fair well as did the doctor. Even Julius was forced to ask Luke for medicine to help quell the tumult in his stomach. At least they reached the landmass and were able to sail on the lee side, where the wind did not strike the ship so fiercely. Rounding the southeast corner of the island, they put in at Fair Havens, a short way from the captain's intended stop at Lasea. Julius thought, "With a name like Fair Havens, this should be a good port to stay awhile in." It was, after all, approaching the very worst part of the year for sailing.

The captain and his men had decided it would be better to sail on to Phoenix. The harbor there had both a southwest and a northwest opening. The captain informed Julius of his plan. Paul, who was sitting nearby with one of the soldiers, stopped a story he was telling about God's sending an earthquake and opening a jail he and another man were in. Julius turned to Paul, for he seemed to have something to say. Paul spoke up firmly, "I believe we are here at the wrong time of the year. If we continue, we will lose not only the ship and the cargo but also our lives. It is truly best that we winter here. We can get provisions readily and sail at the first opportune time in the spring." The captain frowned at him, thinking: "Who does this man think he is telling me, a seasoned captain, how to evaluate this weather? It will be rough but we can make it. After all, I have little to lose since the Roman government has insured my ship against loss." He moved to turn Julius' back to Paul. Julius questioned him about hidden reefs and unlighted coasts and harbors. The Captain kept insisting all the more that the harbor of Phoenix would be better. Besides, he knew this path well. Julius took his advice. Paul shook his head and returned to his story telling.

A gentle south wind began to blow. Thinking all was well, the captain called for the anchor to be weighed. The ship would sail along the shoreline. Paul and Luke sat talking, the wind blowing into their faces. Julius lounged nearby. One of his men and the other guards gambled at the other end of the deck. Paul was recounting the impression that a man's death had on himself. As Julius listened he heard, "I didn't know what it was at the time but that feeling of bewilderment I had as I stood watching Stephen be stoned while I held the cloaks of those stoning him wrenched me. For days it warted me. At night I would have nightmares. I would be throwing stones and Stephen would be saying 'Don't lay this to his charge, Father.' Then he would look at me. I would awake in a cold sweat. Now, I know it was God dealing with me. At the time, I just considered it a horrible dream.

"In an effort to escape the nightmare, I joined a group who had determined to go to the synagogues in Damascus to seek out any who might have believed in this heresy. The high priest eagerly gave us letters saying we could arrest any such believers and bring them back to Jerusalem to be imprisoned. Surely becoming more active in the cause of Jewry would please God. As you know, Luke, God had a purpose for my being at that stoning."

The ship had been sailing less than an hour when a northeaster hit, struck from behind the island. The ship began to pitch. The crew scurried about, attempting to secure the ship. Julius moved Paul and Luke to the center of the deck. "We should go below," he thought. The tiller had its way, for the captain could not force it against the mighty wind. The ship ran under the lee of a small island marked Caudal on his map. The lifeboat ropes seemed to loosen. Crewmen attempted to secure them.

The storm's force tossed the ship. "We must not get blown onto the sandbars of Syrtis," the captain ordered. "Pass ropes under the ship to hold it together. Then lower the anchor. Perhaps we can get farther out to sea." The crew worked swiftly as they tried to keep their footing. "Strike the sails to lessen our speed. That should help us to stay away from those sandbanks and quicksand." All day, the storm battered the boat. No one ate. Paul and Luke sat in an attitude of prayer. At times they spoke encouragingly to crew members as they passed by. Julius was ready to run aground, anything to get his feet back on land.

No sun rose the next morning. The captain ordered the crew to throw some of the cargo overboard. None questioned his decision; better to lose the pay for some of the cargo than to lose one's life. How that prisoner and doctor could be so calm puzzled Julius. He guessed the prisoner knew the charges against him were severe enough that he had no chance surviving anyway. Drowning here would be just as well. As for the doctor, Julius decided he might be crazy to be so calm. Two days of this weather was enough.

The third morning came. The storm raged on. The ship was driven about even more. The captain yelled, "Throw the tackle overboard." Some of the crew wondered at the order but obeyed. Again, Julius had to ask Luke for medicine. He could not eat; his stomach ached unmercifully. Though Paul and Luke ate little, they seemed to have no stomach problems. The saltiest of the seamen weren't eating.

As the morning of the thirteenth day of storming dawned, the sea still tossed in lead colored waves. The crewmen began to murmur about the ill-advised undertaking. The desire to make that bit of extra money which had made them take this last job of the sailing season had long ago vanished. After one sailor cried out, "We are all going to die," the rest echoed and re-echoed that fact.

Paul, upon hearing such talk, spoke to them. "You see you should have taken my advice and not sailed from Crete. Don't give up because all of us will live through this. The ship will be destroyed, not us. Last night an angel from my God, the only true God, spoke to me. For believing and teaching about my God, I am being sent to Rome. The angel said, 'Be not afraid, Paul. You must carry God's message to Caesar in the form of your trial. God will spare you and all who are on the ship with you.' You can trust my God to be faithful to His promise. Keep up your courage. We will run aground. Only the ship will be lost. Luke and I have been praying for you."

The crew gathered in knots as they mulled over what Paul had said. Most became heartened at the news they would not die. Some wondered about the God Luke and Paul had been praying to. Others railed on and on about the captain's poor judgment. When one of the crew jumped him about his decision to sail, the captain replied, "I have sailed through here many times as the last trip of the season. Never have I had such a problem. Never, I tell you." Secretly, he was heartened at hearing he wouldn't die. A mutiny and plank walking could have been his lot.

Still the storm did not stop. The boat pitched deeper into the rough waters. All were still awake at midnight. Something was changing in the sounds. Land sounds! The crew rushed to take soundings. The water was still deep, one hundred and twenty feet. A bit later, the soundings taken were ninety feet. They could be headed for rocks. The captain ordered four anchors to be dropped. The minutes until daylight crept by.

Fearing for their lives, some crewmen who just knew that balded Jew knew nothing began to plot their escape. They would put out the lifeboat in a pretense of putting down anchors from the bow. Paul had been watching them and realized what they were about. He warned the centurion, "If all of us do not stay on ship, you will not be saved." Julius spoke to the captain. The captain order the ropes to the lifeboats cut, allowing them to slip away. "Now, none of us have a chance," one of the miscreants charged.

As dawn neared Paul urged the captain to have the crew eat. "They will need food to survive. Remember, not a one of them will be lost." Exhibiting his faith in what he had urged, Paul took some bread, bowed his head and gave thanks to God for it and for their safety. He then broke a piece off and began to eat. Luke took some. Julius reached out for some. The captain looked across the water. He held out his hand and Paul placed bread in it. The crew began to follow suit. After eating, they felt better. With their spirits raised, some of the crew suggested to the captain that getting rid of the rest of the grain onboard might enhance their chances of safety.

As daylight came, the captain saw they were close to land. A bay with a sandy beach lay ahead of them. If they could run aground here, they might be safe. He ordered the anchors lifted and the foresail hoisted to the wind to make a run for the beach. The bow struck the sandbar and held fast; the stern was still pounded by the rough sea. The soldiers said all the prisoners should be killed to keep them from escaping. Julius ordered them not to do so. He reminded them that Paul had assured them they would be saved. He was amazed that he had recommended what his prisoner had said.

Taking over from the captain, Julius ordered, "If you can swim, jump into the water and swim for shore. Those who can't swim, jump in and grab a piece of debris and float to shore. You will be able to make it." He ordered each soldier to assist one prisoner each to shore. He saw to Paul and Luke. Loosening Paul's chains, Julius told him to jump in and swim. Luke swam, holding his medicine kit above the water. Julius, taking only one chain, swam with powerful strokes. He arrived at the shore in time to aid some of the wearier crewmen to their feet. Because the captain knew the Roman government had his ship insured, he was not worried that it had broken up.

Immediately islanders gathered. They set about building a fire in a sheltered place. The rain and wind had not subsided. The soldiers kept their prisoners in a small group to avoid their escaping. Paul and Luke helped the crew gather brush and wood for the fire. The other soldiers wondered at Julius' allowing Paul the freedom to help. They noised among themselves that Julius was setting himself up to have an escaped prisoner. As Paul placed his wood on the fire, a snake that had been in the bundle, bit him and held on. The islanders' eyes grew wide, for they expected Paul to drop dead momentarily. Certainly he was a murderer found out! Instead, Paul shook the snake off and continued to gather wood. The islanders kept watching him, just knowing he would die. When he didn't, they determined he was a god.

About that time, Publius, the chief official of the island, arrived. He welcomed the captain and Julius. "Bring your people to my home. We can put you two and those prisoners of Julius in the main house. The rest of the group, we can lodge in the barn. I have food and potable water enough." The captain and Julius quickly agreed to the arrangement. The sailors, soldiers, and other prisoners were content with any quarters that were not pitching about.

Publius told them as they neared his estate that his father was ill. His fever was caused by dysentery. After they were settled, Paul asked Julius to seek permission for him to go to the father. Julius wonder about Paul's going when Luke was the doctor. Nevertheless, he asked Publius. Publius and Julius accompanied him. The only other person allowed in was the servant who had agreed to nurse the older man. Upon reaching the man's bedside, Paul bowed his head to pray. After praying, Paul put his hand on the patient and he was healed. Publius praised Paul. Paul told him "It was not I who healed him. I was only God's instrument." Publius asked to know more about this God who could heal through other people. Julius was puzzled by it all.

The servant ran to get some food for the healed man. As he garnered items for the tray, he told the kitchen staff what had happened. And then they told other persons on the staff and estate. A trickle of ill persons began arriving. Paul healed them in his God's name. Luke, the real doctor, stood by, praying or watching.

It would be three months before the Alexandrian ship in port for the winter would sail. After lodging three days at Publius, Julius found a place for his entourage to wait out the time. Soon anyone who was ill was brought to the place. Some brought food "to pay for the healing"; others brought coins. All were most grateful and promised to help provide for the group until they could get underway. Many of them asked Julius to forget about taking Paul on to Rome. Paul heard about this and told them, "No, I must go to Rome." Julius pondered over Paul's response. If he had a chance to escape from appearing before Caesar as a prisoner, he would jump at the chance. Paul seemed unflustered by such an action.

Finally the day to sail for Rome came. As the little party came down to the second grain ship they were to board, they noted the twin gods Castors and Pollux on the bow. From all that Julius had seen in the past months, it seemed a bit ironic that they should be sailing under gods other than Paul's. He was evaluating all that he heard in Paul and Luke's conversations about their

God. He knew that many of those who had come for healing had believed in The Way.

Many of the islanders, including Publius and his father, came to see the ship depart. They waved as long as they could see the ship. As some turned away, they rejoiced in Paul's coming and the healing he had done. Others rejoiced not only in the healing of their bodies but also of their souls.

"The water is fine." That statement was repeated over and over by the crew and soldiers as the ship made its way toward Syracuse. After three days of uneventful sailing, they reached port. A small amount of cargo was unloaded. The next morning the ship sailed for Rhegium. Several of the crew spent time asking Paul questions about his God. They wanted to add this God to the gods they already worshipped. After all, plugging all gaps in one's gods might prove more profitable. Paul still insisted they needed only to take this Christ who had died for their sins as their only hope of salvation. As he tried to get them to realize they would not always be out of harm's way, he assured them this Christ was constantly interceding with God for them. A god they could understand, but a Savior who interceded puzzled them. Were not priests of the various gods to do that for them? Though Julius attempted to look disinterested in the whole of the God/god conversations, he listened closely. He watched Paul and Luke carefully for indications of magic or sorcery but saw none.

A huge crowd met the ship at Rheguim. That was not surprising, since the Romans met every grain ship from Egypt, the bread basket of the Roman Empire, with much rejoicing. As they left Rhegium, a south wind came up. At first Julius feared a storm like the earlier one that had stranded them. At least they were in Italian waters and close to shore. The wind, however, was soft and pushed the ship more quickly toward the next stop, Puteoli. It only took a day to put in to Puteoli. The ship was not required to lower its top sails, a privilege reserved only for these ships that brought grain from Egypt. Julius, though anxious to get on to Rome to see his mother and family, agreed they could stay a week with the followers of The Way, who had met them at the landing. He would much rather have gone on because the town reeked of sulphur. "We'll smell like rotten eggs when we leave," he thought. The other soldiers and their prisoners pressed on for Rome.

Julius knew he needed the rest he could have here, for sailing was not his way of moving about. Too, the followers did not object at all to having a Roman centurion and three Roman soldiers in their midst. How they had found out that Paul was coming to Rome was anyone's guess. Maybe someone had come over from Macedonia after Aristarchus had arrived there. He was not, however, in the group. Later in the week, Julius asked about him. One Jonas told him Aristarchus had gone to Iconium as a missionary to serve God. "To serve God? So that is what they call ones who have chosen to go about telling about this God," thought Julius.

Despite the stench of the sulphur, the week passed all too quickly for Julius. He had marveled at stories he heard Paul tell about his concern over the influence of "the world" on the church at Corinth. Paul declared the wealth of many in the congregation, pagan customs all around, and the factions in the church hurt that church's witness. He heard several more times the story of what Paul called his conversion to The Way. Paul had noted that as he had gone about persecuting Christians, the presence of this Christ hovered in the places that he had taught. Such presence had angered Paul. Paul told of a friend named Barnabas who brought him from Tarsus to Antioch and their preaching by the beautiful fountains there. He spoke of his desire to go to Spain. In Julius' mind that was wishful thinking. Paul wasn't going to get off easy when he faced Caesar! The trip to Rome had to be made Julius reminded himself. Yet when Paul asked that they delay until after the Jewish Sabbath, Julius agreed.

Finally, the party set out on the Appian Way. As they walked along the cemented stones, Paul began to tell about his appearance before Felix and the two years he met with Felix. As they neared the Forum of Appius, Paul shook his head and said, "One of the reasons Felix kept talking with me was he wanted to be given a bribe. I probably could have been released for a price if I had done so. That just isn't our way. Never though did Felix become a believer." Julius was about to say, "I haven't been with you two years, Paul, but you have nearly persuaded me to become a believer," when a rather large group of men rounded a curve in the road. As they approached, one shouted, "Is that you Paul?" The group had come down from Rome toward the Forum of Appius just to accompany Paul to Rome. They were eager to visit with Luke, for they knew he would give them details of the voyage, details Paul would think inconsequential.

Seeing the group delighted Paul. Immediately, he bowed his head and thanked God for their coming. As they walked on passed the aqueduct Claudia, his step seemed lighter, for the company from Rome had brought along some Jewish delicacies in a basket. Paul eagerly ate some. "How good to have some home food," he repeated over and over. Julius noted that the men from Rome had bowed their heads as the food was served. They had not waited for Paul to ask them to do so.

As they approached Rome, two soldiers, who had been sent down to take over the prisoner if he ever arrived, rode up on their horses. They carried the orders as to the housing prepared for keeping Paul prisoner. Since Paul was a Roman citizen, he was to be in a small house with a soldier as watchman. Because Julius outranked the newly arrived soldiers, he said he and his men would go along, too. Julius knew there would actually be three soldiers on duty during a twenty-four hour period. He would have to petition for Luke to remain in the household with Paul. Perhaps some of the group that had come would provide food for Luke. Personally, Julius would want to look in on Paul occasionally. He wanted to be sure of what believing in Paul's God really meant to him as a Roman. If Paul as a Jew yet a Roman citizen could be a believer as well as Luke, a Gentile yet not a Roman could believe in this God, could a Roman who was from greater Rome be a believer?

53 A. D.

Leadra had her youngest grandchild with her. Julius held the youngster for a few minutes before his nurse came to claim him for his nap. Leadra looked at Julius, shaking her head. "Son, you'd make such a good father. Why is it you cannot find a suitable mate? The girls your age are married or betrothed. You'll be left to choose a bride far too young, one who knows little about the comforts needed by a man of your stature and age."

"My dear mother, just be patient. I just can't seem to settle on a bride. I have barely escaped all your friends' marriageable daughters. They have found others. Perhaps I'll never marry."

"Never marry! Julius, we have been through this many times. You will need someone to look after your needs other than a valet. I am getting too old to look after you. Your brothers have given me such lovely grandchildren. Will you give me none?"

"Now, Mother," he teased, "is that all you want of me—grandchildren? You know how monstrous Cletus can be. Remember the stories of my own impishness you have told time after time." Rising he said, "I must be going to check on the soldier who is guarding this Paul."

"You aren't staying for dinner tonight? Son, how do I know you are eating well?"

"Mother, I am not too lean, am I? You sound like you want to fatten me like a calf for the kill."

Shaking her head, Leadra walked with him to the door. A servant brought his sword, which he strapped on. After pressing her cheek to his, he walked to his mount. Off he rode. As he reached the small house on Caesar Street, he saw a young woman and a young boy leaving. The woman looked up at him, pulled the boy close, and hurried away. She was a Jewess he could tell. The boy, however, had neither the face nor the build of a Jew. He put the reins over the post and walked into the small courtyard.

Marselius greeted him cordially as usual. "I see you had a visitor."

"No, she was Paul's visitor. They talked at length about her having come to Rome to seek a better life for her son. From what I gathered, she is alone and his sole support. She is of that same group Paul is. She had some letters from Jerusalem friends for him. He is reading them now."

"Things are fine here? "

Marselius nodded. "It was good of you to come by, sir. Was there any particular reason?"

"No, I just came from a short visit with my mother. You know how mothers are when they have an unmarried son my age. She was after me again to find a bride. No doubt she has found another girl she wants me to meet. I escaped as soon as I could. I'm off. Your relief should be arriving soon so you can get home to dinner with your family."

As Julius left, Marselius mulled over Julius' lack of a real home of his own. Staying in the best military quarters was not his idea of a comfortable life, not when one could have a sweet wife to look after one's every need and children to love and play with.

That night Julius dreamed of his days in Palestine with the occupation troops. He sat up, alarmed. That young woman at Paul's quarters was the woman—the girl—he had forced to come to his quarters. He had thought he had seen her before. The boy! What about the boy? It came back to him. She had not taken his money. Had she conceived that night? Was that his child? The build more Roman like than Jewish. Marselius had gathered from her talking with Paul that she was here to find work to support that boy. Within him stirred feelings he did not recognize at all. In the morning he would return to Paul's house to find where she was staying. If this. ... Julius slept no more. The cock crew and he readied himself for the day. His boy, hearing him stirring, rushed in with shaving water and towels. "Master, what would you like for breakfast?"

"Nothing. I'll find something later. I have a task right now."

"Did a messenger come and I slept through? I'm so sorry, Sir."

"No, no. I just remember a duty I need to complete. I will return later if my schedule permits. Have my quarters clean and my bath laid." At this point, Julius did not want to deviate too much from his regular routine.

The boy called for his master's mount. Julius grinned at him and even waved. What was his master about? He never acted like this.

At Paul's house, Julius dismounted and tossed the reins to Caius, Paul's guard at this hour. Caius was ready to go to his own house. He had slept well, for Paul really never needed a guard. He needed secretaries much more.

Paul was on his knees, praying. He mentioned names Julius had heard him call while they were on the seas. Julius bowed his head and waited. One could at least respect this man and his God for whom he was imprisoned. Paul cut his prayers short, sensing Julius' presence. He could pray on the way to the place Julius might be taking him.

"Good morning, Paul. Does all go well?" Julius said in an anxious tone.

"Ah, good morning. Yes, all goes well." Paul wondered about the anxiety in Julius' voice.

"Yesterday you had visitors, a Jewess and a small boy. Where might I find them?" Paul had long ago learned Julius way a gentle man, but he feared for the girl and her boy. Could Julius have marked her as a possible Christian for arrest or the lions' den? What should he answer? He knew Julius could find her even if he didn't tell where she was. He would tell him. As he told, he would be praying for her safety.

"She is staying with my friend Aquila and his wife Priscilla for the time being. She is looking for work. Priscilla has offered to watch the boy while his mother works. Perhaps you know of a place she can work?"

Julius ignored Paul's question. "And where does Aquila live?"

"At the southern edge of a property owned by Simon of Nazareth, there is a small house. You will find a tentmaker's sign hanging over the door. Since Priscilla and Aquila have no children, they want the little family to stay with them. They will teach the boy tent making. Priscilla feels the girl is too delicate to do the hard work of tent making. She hopes for her to get a position as a gentle woman's maid."

Thanking Paul and turning quickly, Julius greeted Marselius, who had come to stand his watch. Caius was ready to leave. Julius asked him if he knew the way to Paul's friend Simon of Nazareth. Caius replied as he pointed toward the east, "He may be the Jew who lives next to the tentmakers. Check with him." Julius mounted his horse and turned him toward the area of Rome Caius had indicated. "What would Julius want with Simon?" Marselius asked Caius. Caius just shrugged his shoulders and left. He would stop by the baker's for some sweet rolls as a treat for his boys.

The horse bearing Julius trotted along at a stead pace for fifteen minutes. "The woman and child had walked a long distance to see Paul," he thought. "Of course, she had letters for Paul. They must have been important for her to have walked so far."

As he approached the street Caius had indicated, he spotted the tentmaker's sign above the door of a small house. Until now, he had not considered how he would approach the girl. He didn't even know her name. Oh, he would pretend he needed a tent made. Perhaps she would be in the shop. As he dismounted, the boy ran out of the house. "Mister, what a great horse!"

"Peter, Peter, come back and finish your breakfast. Why have you left the table in such a—" The young woman burst through the doorway. She stopped short. Then, she attempted to tuck Peter behind her as the Jewish women had tucked their children behind them when he had met them on the streets of Jerusalem.

Lowering her eyes, she said, "I will send Aquila. Come, Peter. Come."

"Can't I look at the horse, Mother? He is so beautiful." Aquila was at the door by this time.

"Sir," he said, "Good morning. Come into the shop." Peter's mother was pulling him back into another room. The lad kept looking back at the horse.

How was Julius going to explain his visit to this Jewish man who might be the woman's kinsman? He knew from Paul that this man was not the child's father, perhaps not even a kinsman. These people of The Way looked out for one another, kin or no kin. How would he get to talk with her alone?

Aquila looked quizzically at the Roman. How handsome he was even if he were a Roman. Looking at his insignia, he recognized that he might be ordering a large number of tents for a Roman campaign. That task would not be the place Aquila would want his tents used but one did not get to choose the places his wares were used.

Julius decided he should just be straightforward. "I have no need for tents as of now. What I would like is a chance to talk with that young woman if I may?" He could not believe he was asking permission of a Jew but he was.

Aquila looked at him, quite surprised. "I suppose if she wants to talk with you." What was the purpose here? Eunice had been out of the house only once, yesterday to deliver letters to Paul. Priscilla had wanted him to take them but Eunice had insisted they were her charge to deliver in person. She had said nothing about talking with a Roman soldier.

Aquila lifted the curtain to the inner room. He called to Eunice, who came quickly. "Eunice, this soldier would like to talk with you." She lowered her eyes. "You may talk here in the shop if you like. Perhaps God has answered our prayers about work for you." She slipped through the doorway. Aquila moved into the inner room and called to Peter to hurry with his breakfast so they could take a walk before a customer arrived.

Once they were alone, Julius could only stare at Eunice. That name suited her; his mother would like it. What was coming over him? Did it matter that his mother would like her name? "Were you really on the way to care for your aunt?" By the question, Eunice knew positively who he was. She shook her head up and down. She dare not look at him. He moved toward her. She

23

moved behind a chair to grasp its back. "I won't hurt you, Eunice. The boy, is he part Roman?" Again, she nodded. "Could he be mine?"

She looked up at him with fright in her eyes. "Yes." Fiercely she added, "But he is mine. You cannot have him. I have suffered too much ill repute for you to take him." Almost desperately, she added, "I will pray for my God to strike you dead if you even attempt to take him." Her eyes widened as she realized what she had said.

"No, I won't take him from you. I do want to see him. Eunice, I am now a Christian. I have been in contact too long with Paul for him not to convince me that The Way is the only way of life. Even my mother does not know about my acceptance. She thinks I am still Romanish in my behavior. So much is she convinced of my ill behavior that she constantly pushes me to marry and have children." Eunice looked up at Julius in disbelief. He continued. "How many Roman soldiers have you known?"

Dropping her eyes again, she whispered, "None other."

How he had wronged her. His old life tasted so bitter now, even bitterer than before today. Had God taken him away the next day to punish him? She had suffered criticism when he had been the one who had forced her to bed. Even if he had stayed in Jerusalem he probably would never had seen her again. He needed some time to think.

"May I come again? Will you not run away?"

"Yes, you may come when Aquila and Priscilla appoint a time, for this is their home."

"I will come back," he said gently. As he turned to go, she lifted her tear-filled eyes. He longed to dry them but dared not trust himself this day. Strange feelings kept washing over him.

As he rode away, Peter came running into the shop to join his mother at the door. "Mother, will he come back so I can see his horse?"

:"Yes, Peter, he will come back. Of that, today I am certain."

NAAMAN

Naaman's household was different. It was different because Naaman and Lois were different from the other Syrian officers and their families.

Perhaps that was the chief reason the King of Aram choose Naaman as his sole companion when the time to go to the temple of the god Rimmon came.

He took Naaman with him to help him up and down, for he was getting feeble. Perhaps that is why the King listened when Naaman came with the story of the prophet in Israel. Perhaps that is why Naaman was Commander-in-chief of the Syrian armies and seemed to be unbeatable in battle. Of course, Naaman was different because he was a leper; but his wife was different too, for she had not told him to leave because of his leprosy.

When the Syrians had carried off some Israelite captives, among them was a young girl named Rhoda. As Naaman looked at her, he saw the perfect maid for his wife. Naaman saw to it that Rhoda was brought into his tent and cared for. Fear crept into Rhoda's heart, for often the Syrians raped young Israelite girls. As Naaman spoke to her of his many roomed home, of his darling Lois, and of their love for one another, her fears began to fade. This Syrian was unusual. He did want her to be a maid only. Rhoda thanked God then as well as in her usual evening prayers.

Upon their arrival in Damascus Naaman sent Baasha, his servant, with Rhoda to his home. Rhoda's bow delighted Lois. Immediately she sent for bath water and fresh clothes for the tired youngster. A clean Rhoda soon presented herself. Lois explained to her the specific duties she would have: she was to bring fresh goat's milk for Lois at seven each morning; she would then lay out the clothing for the day as Lois' head lady Bathel directed; after Bathel had brought in bathwater, her task would be making the great carved cypress bed; as her mistress walked in the garden, Rhoda would accompany her to bring this blossom or leaf or even a drink from the spring. As Lois recited her list of afternoon activities, the brightest spot for Rhoda was having free time at the precise time her mother had taught her to say her evening prayers. "This is certainly going to be a full day's work," Rhoda thought. "So this is what it's like to be a captive." Opening the door to a small chamber, Lois concluded, "You shall sleep on the bed in there where I can call you at night if I need you.

As the days wore on, Rhoda found her tasks not nearly as heavy as she had perceived them to be. Making the huge bed was pleasant. Lois used only the best perfumes on her linens. And too, Rhoda could run her hands over those smooth white linens and trace the gold thread designs with her fingers. On occasion, Lois let her play in the garden instead of walking behind her.

One day Rhoda looked up from her play to see Lois seated on a bench not too far away. She was wiping her eyes. Had she been crying? Was she crying about the thing Rhoda had heard talk about as she waited for the goat's milk each morning? Was Lois disturbed over Naaman's leprosy? Rhoda knew lepers were outcasts among her people. Apparently they weren't here in Syria.

For several days Rhoda paid close attention to Lois as they walked and rested in the garden. She began to think, "Perhaps my mistress might listen to me about Naaman's illness." Lois had taken her suggestions several times about different combs for her long blonde hair. Especially had Lois been pleased with her comb suggestion the evening Naaman and Lois had eaten with the King. One day, she approached Lois. "Ma'am," she whispered, giving that odd little bow which so amused Lois. "Ma'am, I wish my master would go to see the prophet in Samaria. He would heal him of his leprosy."

Lois blinked and looked at Rhoda. "What did you say?" Rhoda repeated herself. "What is his name? Where does he live? What does he charge?" All these questions young Rhoda could not answer. She could only tell Lois that her mother had often told her of the prophet who could and would heal. Lois framed Rhoda's face in her slim hands. "Rhoda, think hard. If you can remember more, tell me quickly." Rhoda thought but could not think of any more information.

That evening Lois reported her conversation with Rhoda to Naaman. "A Samarian prophet who can heal one of leprosy? Where in Samaria?" Lois had such few details. Naaman called for Rhoda. She repeated her little information. Both adults pressed for more, but Rhoda could only repeat, "He does live in Samaria. My mother told me so."

The next day Naaman gave his scant bit of information to his king. Unhesitatingly, the King declared King Jehoram would certainly know the whereabouts of such a wondrous prophet. He would know such a person if he existed in his kingdom. "You are to go to King Jehoram, Naaman. I'll give you a letter of introduction. And you'll have gifts, both gold and silver for him. Oh, to have you whole!"

All Naaman's household hurried with the preparations to aid the master In preparing to go to Samaria. The suits of clothing, provisions and the money sacks—all were readied. When Rhoda appeared for Lois' goat's milk, the staff quizzed her, pressing to know much more than Rhoda herself knew. The King's servant brought the important letter of introduction which Naaman quickly placed in his bags. As Lois wished him well, Rhoda ran to her small chamber .to pray for the prophet to be found and for him to heal Naaman.

Day after day Lois, Rhoda, and the rest of the household waited. The minutes went by so slowly. Rhoda often felt Lois' eyes upon her as if asking, "Were you right, little girl? If you weren't. . . If the prophet is dead.? Was your mother repeating a story of old?" Yet Lois said none of these things to Rhoda. The heat of the land seemed almost oppressive. Lois seemed to require more slips of water from the spring in the garden. After several days, Rhoda, like everyone else, wanted only to scan the horizon toward Samaria.

After twelve days, a cloud of dust kicked up. A messenger? No, a whole retinue was coming. Surely Naaman was healed or dead they hurried so! The mule cart was loaded with something, for it traveled slower than the main party. As the party came closer, Lois caught sight of Naaman's banner. He was still alive. Oh, that he were healed!

Naaman reported to the King first. He did so hurriedly, begging the King's patience for a complete account until he had gone to Lois in person. His news was such that he wanted to tell her. The King granted permission. Naaman mounted his horse quickly. Of course, the news of his cure had flown through the streets so Lois had heard; but she wanted to hear for sure from Naaman. When he arrived, she stood at the entrance to the garden. Immediately he put out his hands to her. She took them, turning them over. She pushed back his sleeves. His hands and arms were clear. "And my whole body is just like these hands and arms. Lois, I'm healed. Rhoda was right. Her mother was right. The prophet can heal." Pulling Lois into his arms, Naaman held her tight. At that moment Naaman spotted Rhoda's skirt swish beyond a bush. He called to her. "Where did she go?" he asked.

"Probably to thank her God. Oh, Naaman, she has been so sure, yet not so sure. Often I have seen her creep into her chamber to pray." Naaman looked at Lois.

"That's something we must discuss, Lois."

"Can't it wait until you tell me about the healing?"

"Yes, it can be a part of that story." Naaman went in to greet his household; then he and Lois returned to the garden for his story. Often they were interrupted by well-wishers.

"Lois, as we rode to Samaria I kept wondering why I was on such a goose chase. You know how the dust irritated my leprosy. When we reached King Jehoram he took my letter, read it, and dismissed himself with 'I need to think.' He dismissed himself for three whole days. Lois, I was sure then that Rhoda was wrong, that she might be a part of a trap to capture me in retaliation for our taking captives. I knew he couldn't win anything but I also knew I could get killedI for a false hope. On the fourth day, King Jerhoram summons me to his throne. Smiling broadly, he said he had a servant ready to direct me to one Elisha's house. Well, I thought 'Here's the old run around trick' so I told my men to keep up their guards.

"We followed the servant to this Elisha's house. It was such a little place, not at all what our prophets live in. A servant came out and told me 'Go wash in the Jordan River seven times. You will be cured of your leprosy.'

"Lois, I was furious. Elisha didn't even bother to come out himself. He didn't let me come into his house. A servant brings the message and what a message: to wash in the dirty Jordan River. "Creek" he should have called it. Why the Abana and Pharpar would much better place to wash. I wheeled my horse around and charged away. My horsemen followed. I drew up and they gathered around. Believe me; I gave vent to my anger.

"Thank goodness, my men stayed levelheaded. Aga urged me to at least try the advice. The rest agreed we had come too far not to do such such a simple thing. Apparently they, like me, had figured that before I was healed

I'd have great tasks to do for the prophet's God. We talked for awhile until I cooled down. I had to agree I couldn't get much dirtier dipping in the Jordan than I had on the trip over. We rode to the Jordan. The men dismounted and stood on the bank. I dismounted and waded in. 'Since I'm here,' I thought, 'I thought I better get all wet' so I waded to a deep hole. As I dipped the men counted, 'One, two, three, four, five, six." After each dip I checked but the leprosy was still there. "Seven," they chorursed as I went under the seventh time. Cautiously, I opened my eyes to look at my hands. Clear! Clean! I was healed! We pumped each other's hands, hit each other on the back, laughed, and repeatedly looked at my hands, my arms, my legs. Oh, Lois, being whole is great."

Lois squeezed his arm. "Then you came home?"

"Oh, no. We rode back to the prophet's house. As we neared there, we all realized how skeptical we had been, particularly me. We had quieted down considerably. When we got there, Elisha was in his tiny garden. We dismounted and went to greet him. Lois, without realizing what I was saying—at least at first—I said 'I know there is no God in all the world except your God.' As I heard those words I realized my mouth was saying what my heart had come to know. I repeated 'I know there is not God in all the world except in Israel. As His prophet, accept my gifts.'

"Elisha would not accept the gifts. He insisted God cared for him. Neither he nor his God needed such gifts. Though I urged, he steadfastly refused. I relented, asking if he would give me two mule loads of Israel soil to bring here so I can build and altar on which to worship God. Lois, the carts are coming. We need to pick the choicest place in the garden to build this altar. Always we must worship God, asking His guidance, thanking Him for Rhoda, for Elisha, for healing me."

Lois drew back from Naaman. "Naaman, what about your being required to go with the King when he goes to the temple of Rimmon? That's required. And Naaman, you have to bow before Rimmon as the King does for you say you must assist him as he bows and rises."

Naaman looked at Lois. "I mentioned this to the prophet, asking if God could pardon me since my job requires this as a formality. I will not be worshiping Rimmon, only assisting the king. Elisha said, 'All right,' Lois. He must have been able to read my heart. Lois, I'm, hopeful our king will come to know there is no God in all the world except in Israel and that he, too, will come to worship him."

Lois' eyes gleamed. "I want to worship Him with you, Naaman, for He is God." Naaman drew Lois closer to him.

"I just knew you'd confess Him, too."

"You brought all the money back to the King and the clothing, too?"

"No, it seems that after we started towards home two prophets from Ephraim came to Elisha. They had need of money and clothing; Elisha sent his servant, the one who had come out and told me to dip seven times in the Jordan, to ask for $2,000 and two suits of clothing for them. I readily gave him the clothing and $4,000. I'd have sent all the silver and gold but I thought Elisha would have sent it back. But, Lois, I'm wondering about that. Since Elisha knew my heart about assisting the king in his worship of Rimmon, why didn't he know about the imminent coming of these two prophets and ask for those things while I was there?"

I don't know," Lois answered. "I do know you are home and healed. We have Rhoda to think."

"Yes, let's go find her so I can thank her. I need to tell her about the altar, too. She can share it."

A RIGHT ENCOUNTER

She pursed her lips ever so slightly. Would he ever let that pleat do what it wanted? Must he insist that it turn exactly like the rest on her aqua silk? Was perfect accord necessary? Silks look better flowing. She would have jerked, but he would have been confused. Instead, she gritted her teeth.

That odor? It was like a chem... Another odor, a fragrance, several fragrances, whiffed about her head. Slitting her eyes, she was puzzled by the mistiness that kept creeping in. She squeezed her eyes slightly, hoping the lady standing nearby didn't notice. Something was changing; the mistiness was thickening. It became a mist that could buoy her up. Her body felt lighter. It was almost as though she were moving, then turning.

Opening her eyes completely, she found the mist to be all around; but she was not frightened as she had been when forced to drive her black coupe through fogs. The mist drew her forward toward a mass. The closer she came to the mass the farther it seemed to extend. It seemed endless, extending beyond the not to distant horizon. The mist gently put her down on the mass which seemed cloudlike now.

A figure appeared on the horizon. She wondered who it could be. The figure strode toward her. It was Lew! He stretched out his hand toward her.

"Dar," he said, touching her hand. "Come. I get to take you in. I'm so glad you've finally come."

You look so well," she said, as a puzzled look crossed her face. "So absolutely –In, you said, in where?"

"In to see Him." Taking her offered hand, Lew led the way up the slight incline to the edge of the horizon. Gazing about, she saw nothing different. Then, the horizon began to fall away. Suddenly, she knew where Lew was leading her.

"Is Peter here? Does he really keep the gate? Is that young man Stephen here? Is he still young? What about Leila, Lew? What about her? Lew, what about Momma? Oh, Lew, what about Him?"

"They're here, Dar, just like we knew they would be." And He . . . well, He is all a brother and a father can be."

"Lew, there is no sun but it is light."

"Dar, He told us He would be the Light."

"Why aren't I worried about my hair, my nails, my hem, these pleats? Oh, there are Momma and Corky!" Over one another, other names tumbled out as she waved to various people and called, "See you in an eon."

An eon? She had never used that word before; yet, it had fallen from her lips as though it were an everyday word. Why didn't she stop to visit with these people she had so longed to see again? It certainly wasn't at Lew's insistence that she didn't stop. Why did they keep walking in this direction?

She saw why. It was He! He was sitting on . ...

What He sat on didn't matter. She eagerly joined the group around Him, bowing low and singing songs of priaise to Him from the very heart of her soul.

The mortician's young assistant moved the wreath of snow mums to close the casket. Pleased, he noted that every pleat in the aqua silk shroud now lay in perfect accord.

THE DREAM

I dreamed last night that I was in Heaven

And there I interceded for my son.

"Oh, God," I said as I watched that adult son

Give too little change to a customer

And then pocket the excess.

"Forgive, my son, he needs more than his employer pays."

Then I saw son driving 45 in a zone marked 25 and pled

"God, forgive him, for he is rushing home to be

With his wife and my grandkids."

II

God looked at me with eyes so sad

And said calmly but clearly,

"Dear one, you love your son as I love Mine.

What has your son done for Mine?"

I stammered and I stuttered,

"Well, God, he gets to worship services

At least twice a year

And every Sunday lets his wife and children go to worship You.

He bows his head when prayers are said

In his house or another's.

Surely, God that's quite enough for such loving boy

Who always honors his mom on her birthday

And you on your Son's.

He's only human, God,

You know, You made him human."

III

God looked at me again and said,

"Yes, I made him human so he could think

And choose and he has chosen thusly.

My Son, what did He do for you and for your son?"

I gulped, "He died to give us life above."

IV

I woke, fell to my knees

And begged God's forgiveness

For thinking my son merited special favors

When God had given His

So mine could have life eternal

OLD ZACHARIAS

Old Zacharias gained his one chance

To travel to the temple

To carry out his levitical duty.

His task to light incense before the Lord

To lead in worship of his Lord.

Into the Temple he walked,

Proud that before his death

He would be allowed to prove

His worth as a member of Levi's tribe

So many of his tribesmen never had such a chance

So multiplied they had become.

Donning priestly robes, he took the lighted taper

To burn incense already placed upon the altar.

Into the protected area he went

Worshippers offered prayers to God,

Asking of Him showers of blessing.

Lighting the incense, Zacharias stepped back

To begin his prayers to God,

To the right of the altar appeared an angel,

A phenomenon Zacharias never expected to see.

He froze, startled with fear

His eyes widened; his breath shortened;

His knees they buckled; His hands they trembled.

"Don't be fearful, Zacharias, God's man,"

(He knows my name! He knows my name!)

"Your prayers from times before God has heard

He now honors them"

(Which prayers" flashed through Zacharias' mind)

"Elizabeth, your faithful wife, shall have of you a son

Name him John, the name God has chosen for him."

(A son? A son for Elizabeth and me?)

"A joy he'll be, for you have long waited for him.

Your friends, your family will rejoice with you.

God rejoices with you, for He has found you faithful.

Of this child John God will make a great man.

I warn you, Zacharias,

He must not partake of hard liquor

A Nazarite, too, he must be.

See to it that you instruct him so.

"This babe will be filled with God's Spirit from birth;

He'll be like Elijah, warning the people of their sins.

But, Zacharias, he is not the Messiah, God's promised One.

He shall, instead, prepare the people to accept the Messiah

When He comes."

Zacharias fumbled the tassels on his robe,

Tears welled in his eyes.

"I'm old; Elizabeth is old. Long has it been

Since we could have babes though we have longed

For just one."

The angel gazed at Zacharias. He smiled.

"I am Gabriel, sent to you straight by God.

I bear His news, none of my own.

That news, Zacharias, you question

But God assures through me it is true.

Until the babe is born no voice shall you have.

God isn't forsaking your part in His plan
He just silences you until you name this child John."

Gabriel vanished as quickly as he had come.
Zacharias fell to his knees in awe before God.
A son! He and Elizabeth would have a son,
The son they had so longed for.
He would be a special gift from God, the Lord Almighty.

Out from the altar place, Zacharias came
The worshipers gathered round
To hear the special message he might carry from God.
He could not speak; they wondered at his silence.
What message had God given him in the cloistered place?

In due time Elizabeth found she was with child.
The blessing neither she nor Zacharias quite understood.
They were simple folk. Why had God chosen
To give them this special gift. It seemed impossible.
Oft their hands met; one's smile infected the other,
No words needed.

In time, Mary, Elizabeth's cousin, came from afar
John jumped in Elizabeth's womb when Mary saluted her.

Mary told her she was with child though she had

Known no man.

As the story of the Immaculate Conception was told

Elizabeth and Zacharias marveled more.

The day of Elizabeth's delivery arrived.

Two midwives came;

Zacharias paced without the door, awaiting

News of the babe's safe arrival.

The old midwife placed the newborn in his arms;

He gazed upon his face.

His son, his promised son, was born.

Others gather in to see this babe

Born of too old parentage.

Forgetting Zacharias' voice was dumb, the

Midwife queried,

"And what will his name be?"

Like the others, she was confident he would be named

A good Hebrew name: Abraham, Moses, David, Elijah.

Zacharias handed her the babe;

He picked up a tablet and a marker.

He wrote, "John."

The onlookers gasped, "John? Why that's not a family name.

Neither is it a tribal name. Whatever makes you name him John?"

Zacharias spoke, confusing them more,

"God chose John to be his name before he

Was even conceived."

One rushed to Elizabeth's side

"He is to be named John?"

Elizabeth nodded, "John is to be his name."

Quickly, Zacharias took the babe.

He carried him to Elizabeth.

Both looked at the child with eyes adoring

As they whispered, "John."

THE MISADVENTURES OF
LAURA AND LINDA

I

Laura and Linda were eight and five. To their mother, it seemed that what one could not think of, the other could. Usually, the victim of their collective pranks was Lois, their much older but much wiser sister. She often forgot two heads are better than one.

One hot summer afternoon, the little girls played paper dolls in the dining room by the high room dividers. Linda had her paper dolls on the right side; Laura, the left. Uptown for the paper dolls was the walkway into the living room where the girls were allowed only when they practiced their piano lessons on the upright fruitwood piano or when company came.

Lois always had to practice first because she was the oldest. This day she was wearing the wine with white polka dots dress she had sewn mostly by herself as her 4-H project. White buttons marched up the front of the princess style dress. Beneath the buttons were snaps, for Lois had not yet learned to use the buttonholer on Mother's sewing machine.

As Lois came from the kitchen, she hummed "Drifting," her favorite piece to practice. Neither of the little girls could play that piece yet, for their hands couldn't reach octaves. She glanced at the "children," as she called them as she walked by their paper dolls. "Now," whispered Laura. Each girl grabbed hold of the hem of the 4-H dress. Its row of hidden snaps clicked, clicked, clicked. And there stood Lois, her dress wide open, her panties showing.

Grabbing the front of her dress, she cried, "Mother, they did it again." Laura and Linda rolled in the floor, laughing.

II

Laura and Linda had been anxious for Christmas to come. For them, vacations flew; school crept, especially after Thanksgiving. Both girls had written Santa Claus. Surely he had gotten the letters, for they had read them in the BEACON.. The girls had insisted that Lois, Mother, and Daddy read them. Daddy, in particular, was bound to know Santa Claus personally.

The letters were the usual kind Santa receives. They wanted baby dolls, a brown-eyed blonde for Laura and a blue-eye brownette for Linda. They had asked for something special this year. They wanted big, big tricycles like they had seen at the circus. Lois had not written a letter but she had asked her parents for her very first bicycle and a fur jacket. A rabbit fur jacket! Ah, what a luxury.

Time crept on. Christmas Eve finally came. The tree with its bright balls, tinsel, and lights stood in the front room window. A few small packages lay on the tree skirt. No sign of the asked for treasures could be seen.

Bedtime didn't come soon enough for the girls. Sleep came even slower. Mother and Daddy carried out their usual evening routine. Mother sat in one rocker reading a section of the paper; Daddy in the other. "Back to bed, girls." And I don't want to have to come in there." A few minutes later came "Now, girls, stop talking and go to sleep." Were Mother and Daddy going to sit up so long Santa wouldn't stop?

Christmas morning Santa had come. Lois had a blue Schwin girl's bike and a fur chubby. Laura and Linda had their big baby dolls and they had huge blue tricycles almost as tall as Lois' bike. They wheeled the vehicles out onto the front porch, down the steps and to the sidewalk. The younger girls ran back into the house to bring out their dolls and seat them in the porch swing. Already neighbor kids were gathering to show and tell what Santa had brought. Dolls drew exclamations from the girls: bats, balls, gloves and vehicles drew the boys' attention.

Lois' bicycle was the biggest of the vehicles. The boys had to check it over. She stood in the crotch and said, "Tell me what you want to know and I'll tell or show you." Naturally, they wanted to hear the bell several times. "Turn on the lights" was the next request. The boys had to check both the head and tail lights. "Will the horn toot when the lights are on?" She tried them and they surely worked. "Are you going to get a license plate?" She figured so. All had to grasp the white handle grips and flip the tassels at the ends. As Lois pushed the bike off to the side, an older boy asked Laura a simple question, "Can she ride it?" Laura replied, "I don't know, but she can sure ride a tricycle."

III

The big blue tricycles attracted attention throughout the younger set in the neighborhood. Soon though the little girls began to toy with the idea they could learn to ride Lois' bike. Sure enough, they easily conquered the knack of riding on two wheels instead of three.

One day, the front tire was a bit low so they took out the air pump from Daddy's tool stash. After much huffing, they got the tire aired to their estimation of the right pressure. Linda ran into the house to ask if they could cross the street to ride down the long block. Returning with a permission granted answer, she hopped on the seat and Laura straddled the crotch. She walked the bike across the street and then tried to start pumping. After wobbling a bit, she got the bike going. Halfway down the block, something went boom. The front tire had blown out. Linda fell off to one side. Laura fell into the handle bars. Wide-eyed they looked at each other. How would they ever get the bike home? What would big sister say? What would Mother say?

They thought over the situation. One could go get the Red Flyer wagon so they could haul it home. Both of them could go but someone might get the bike. The verdict: Laura would straddle the crotch and lift the handle bars high enough to get the tire off the ground. Linda would push on the back rack to roll the back tire. Turning the bike around they started off. Linda pushed too fast so the seat kept hitting Laura the back and the pedals whacked her ankles. Because Laura's arms tired quickly, they had to rest. Linda stood with her arms crossed and her lips pursed. When they had to stop a second time, Linda decided she should hold the handle bars. Naturally, Laura pushed too fast and Linda tired. Back and forth they traded, each getting grumpier.

Lois saw them coming and ran to meet them. "My bike! What have you done to my bike?" Each younger girl accused the other of airing the tire too full. Mother quickly settled the argument by putting the bike in the garage as she said, "I believe this is where this bike will stay for two weeks. Maybe those trikes are for all three of you. Linda and Laura, you will willing let Lois ride one of them any time she wants."

"What a pill," griped Linda, "to have to share your wheels with a big sister.

Laura answered, "At least we can't air our tires up."

MUD PACKS

As a teenager, my older sister had quite a problem with acne. She tried every kind of mask known to her and every new one she read about in magazines. One brand I recall was Edna Wallace Hopper Mudpack. In winter she would no more than get the beauty treatment glopped on—white, ghostly white—when it would be her turn to run to the coal house for more coal to keep the heater fired up. She would look each way down the dirt road for signs of traffic. If she saw no cloud of dust, she was off at top speed, the coal bucket whacking her legs with each step. Invariable, just as she was half way on the return trip, a pickup would appear out of nowhere, slow down, and its occupants would stare. Well, I not only tried some of her mudpack but I've also tried body packs. And these body packs have occurred since my marriage to a certain farmer whose sole reason—I am positive about this—for marrying was to have a farm hand.

My first true mud pack was well mixed with manure. One of the heifers was attempting to calf. She had problems. My husband insisted we run her into the chute and head gate to assist her. The fact that he had somewhat of a makeshift setup did not deter him. Neither did the fact that the mud in that chute was ankle deep because a spring rain had been falling for two days. We ran her into the chute. He attached the pulling ropes to the calf's front feet and yelled, "Pull!" He pulled; I pulled. When the calf plopped in the mud, the tension on the rope relaxed. Husband saw what was happening and let go. I plunged head on into the mixture of mud and manure. Remember no cow forgets to have a bowel movement when she delivers. I muttered all the way to the house epithets not at all complimentary to Husband nor his beloved heifer nor her newborn.

A few years later I inherited my mom's Troybilt rototiller. For some forgotten reason, Husband stored it in the hay barn inside the cow lot. Again, spring rains had fallen for several days; the garden however had drained well. We decided we could do the preparatory work needed for planting. He manhandled the tiller out the door to the cow lot. Yes, there was another gate that opened in to grassed soil. Husband gassed the tiller up and checked the oil. It started on the first try. "Open the gate," he yelled.

I started for the board gate that hadn't been built to open quickly. (Remember your dad's instruction: "Always close a gate you go through.") Husband put the tiller in forward gear. In the ankle deep mud, my rubber boots slipped. I fell face down in—yes you guessed it—well mixed mud and manure. Before he could get the tiller stopped due to his inexperience with it and his laughter, it churned up to my knees. At least I had fallen straddled-legged! He still insists he struggled to hold the tiller back. I wonder.

My sister's mudpacks never did clear up her acne. My packs only made me dirty and ill tempered.

SENSATION

Three times I've had that sensation—

The one where your seat tilts slightly forward,

Your brain flies out a bit, and

Your ears tell you you're pitching out the rest

Of your remains.

The initial descent of any plane,

A roller coaster ride,

And that day I said,

"I do," and sealed my

Earthly plight

To that one man I

Dreamed about all my

Dating life.

March 3, 1986

CHANGES

This cannot be my body reflecting in the mirror:

My body is lithe, slender, smooth.

Hair golden, long,

Face smooth, eyes clear brown;

Smile merry from lips with corners upturned,

One chin. Neck taut and shoulders

Smooth, velvet white.

Firm arms, bust, hips and thighs

Slender waist and ankles

This cannot be my body reflecting in the mirror:

That body is stiff, pudgy, misshapen

Hair dyed golden, frizzed.

Face raisin wrinkled; eyes dark circled, dull.

Smile wry from thinned lips

Three chins, turkey neck,

Shoulders smooth but mushy.

Upper arms flappy, saggy.

Hands age-spotted, veiny.

Waist thick with even thicker hips;

Bulges where curves once dipped.

This cannot be my body reflecting in the mirror.

MY HAIR

I fear I may grow bald.

Bald, not from chemotherapy

Though that is a possibility.

Bald because my hair decides

Just on its own

To fall,

Come out.

Fall out one day around my feet

And lie there on the floor.

I'll look in the mirror

Utterly amazed to see

A scobby white knob

Made up like a mime

Bald.

To become a laugh for some;

A thing of horror for the young..

December 1987

FIFTY-FOUR

I sit on the couch

Ready to read the daily paper.

I look at the front page, pausing to

Read whatever catches my eye

And fancy..

I turn the page.

I become another person, wary

In the middle of column two

I see OBITUARIES, that word.

Furtively I scan to see if

My name is included

And me only fifty-four!

If it's there it will probably be

Followed by teacher—thirty years,

organizations x, y, and z,

church member,

survivors three.

THANK GOD, IT'S NOT THERE TODAY.

Yet, every day—at least since the big five-O—
I've noted more and more
obituaries announce the age of their chief
participants as being fifty plus one through nine.
I'd thought of death before
But those who participated were old.
And I'm not old; I'm prime!

Still, as I page to other
Leaves of the daily,
The athletes are younger
than my son.
Popeye, Betty Boop, and Henry
Have given way to
Tumble Weed, Garfield, and
Doonesbury.
Dick Tracy's still the same;
Charlie Brown and Lucy have
Not changed.
Only Uncle Walt, Seezix and
I have aged.

And I want—wanted to stay prime.

Pre1985

DIVORCE

Too often in marriage, the words
"I love you"
Are pretty words, hollow words
Meant to impress observers.

What is beneath is greed
And ME, the idol ME,
Self satisfied, self serving,
Whiny spoilness, giant I's.

The marriage partner tries,
Seeks to appease, to hide
From family eyes, the hurt,
The sting, the shame.

One day the bands pop!
The partner seeks justice
Through courts and laws.
The pouty partner seeks revenge.

And gets Shylock's pound,

Maybe not in flesh but

In peace and joy of life,

In faith, in justice under the law.

One given because of love;

One chosen because of love

Has been duped, raped.

One worthy of a crown of jewels

Has been shorn,

Shorn even of the

Basic dignity of Man.

Fall 1991

LEFTOVERS

We sit, discarded leftovers:

A tree, bare branched, pleached, barkless,

Once leaves peeked, grew, matured, fell.

Birds mated, nested, sang, migrated.

Web worms feasted.

Those times are no more.

We sit, discarded leftovers:

A 1945 Dodge coupe

Its gray paint marred by rust spots;

Its muffler dragging like a drooping tail feather.

Its windshield out; side windows cracked.

A beauty gone bad.

We sit, discarded leftovers:

A hunched woman in run over shoes;

A teacher, her mind gone;

A sick old man, coughing phlem;

A beggar with his plastic sack,

A homeless soul.

We sit, discarded leftovers,

Buffeted by wind, rain, snow, and time.

PROTEST SONG FOR THE '80'S

It's not right'

It's unfinished,

Undone.

There's not a final wiggle

Where a wiggle's always been.

An overall clad man on the 'back porch,"

A platform for politicians to

Whistle stop on.

It's not right!

It's unfinished,

Undone.

A train without a little red

Caboose and a man to

Wave to all the drivers

Stopped here.

A train that isn't finished

Isn't right.

THE PHONE

Some people praise the phone

As Bell's gift to man.

A gift?

Mortician comes in dead of night

"You're to call the VA Hospital."

"He's dead. Died at ten. We just have gotten time

To call."

It is two.

Halloween, a spook party, a pumpkin cake, a ring.

One touch on the elbow.

"It's about your mom.

She died last night

Or early this morning."

Eastertide, a six months' grandchild gnaws on

Floppy bunny's ear. A ring.

"It's for you, Son."

"Oh, no." He turns to wife.

"It's your dad. He's gone.

He died in his chair. Mom was on the phone and … ."

Memorial weekend. Summer's starting time: leisure,

sun, fun.. A ring.

"Grab that phone."

"A motorcycle accident. And sister? Thank God."

Turning, "A car broadsided them. He's dead.

She's hurt but not badly."

A ring. Summer '89.

Again a message rung to me.

"He's dead. A car wreck."

A life of great promise erased.

A gift? Bell's gift to man?

More like a dirge for me.

(Randy Phillips had been killed in a car wreck at Perkins. 8/20/89)

MEMORY WORK

One day he said his memory work

"My way of life has fallen into the sewer...."

His eyes twinkled as he paused to

Watch my face.

Would it cloud?

Would it smile?

Would it be passive?

Years later I stopped by him as he lay

In a doorway.

He looked up; the old twinkle gone from

His eyes.

"My way of life is fallen into the ....

He choked on "sewer,"

Said earlier in jest to tease teacher,

To defy Shakespeare; to thumb his nose

At culture.

Said in jest at learning;

Said now in truth ending.

MIRRORS

They mirror American women.

They really do: those who work

In all the quaint places we

Visit on our vacations and

holidays.

Those women dressed in

Colonial costumes, turning

Out Williamsburg sugar cookies,

To home to laundry, unswept floors

And dirty dishes.

Those workers who sliced the

Mountains of flaming tomatoes

On which you commented.

"Aren't these just mar-vee-lous!"

Mow lawns, clean garages, and sweat.

The sweet young things who cheer the

Cowboys on

Have financial problems, grocery

lists, and stuffy nose just like

all the avid fans.

And that bonneted woman, hoeing the rows of beans

Yes, the bonneted woman who waved at us as

We passed by

has heartaches.

Today her son, once a strapping youth,

A youth who learned the joy of

Plunging sharp knives in hog bellies

Was executed

For plunging a sharp knife into his girl.

He learned that on this typical Kentucky farm

From that bonneted woman.

6/26/86

OUR LIVES

We're from the WWII generation of preteens/teens

Who declared, "No man shall ever fool us

As Hitler did the Nazis, as emperor worship did the

Japanese.

We know the score; we can't be fooled."

Standing on the brink of sixty, we eat those words—

Words that crumble like stale crackers,

Words bitter sweet, sour sweet.

After graduation we strode off to cold war peace, college, jobs.

We married, bought a houseful of furniture for $199.95—

Enough the advertisers touted to carry us through until

The firstborn comes,

Only to find visiting relatives quickly took

Our one bed when proffered,.

Only to find fat uncles and plump aunts broke matchstick

Chairs beyond repair.

The first born arrived 9 ½ months later,

Just before the temperature gauge on the apartment-sized range

Began to heat to 500 when set on 250,

Arrived so soon because we were fooled by passion when we

Couldn't afford a condom or a gel,

Arrived to cut our funds a quarter because

Breast feeding was out; Similac was in.

Because patriotism thickened our blood—Had we not grown

Up on the "Marines Hymn" and "Praise the Lord and Pass

The Ammunition"—

Young fathers joined the march to Korea to keep this land free

And to augment the family budget.

Nine months later another family heir broke water,

Wrecking even more the family budget.

We paid down on our first home, a GI Joe home like all the

Others on the block, on neighboring blocks, in

neighboring towns.

Homes with pocket hanky yards, clothes lines, two stoops;

One car garages which soon became our woodworking project—a den.

We were "old married folks" by now.

Number three was on the way, a whole two and a half years

After number two, thanks to Korea and a little learning.

Frankie Avalon and Sonic were too young for us.

But we were still young enough to be persuaded a monthly TV

Payment was a must.

The sixties arrived with hippies, flower children and Elvis:

All scandalous, all selling bills of goods we knew better

Than to buy.

JFK's "Ask not what your country can do for you" played sweetly

To our thirty-four year-old minds.

We'd reared our children to join the Peace Corps, not the army.

They'd go to battle ignorance and poverty abroad;

Then they'd come home to be as famous as Elvis with the

Pelvic swing.

We bought another house, moved out of the old neighborhood of

Grilling hamburgers every Friday night

To a new neighborhood where booze and wife swapping were fads.

We wondered why our kids chose peace signs and flowers

Instead of the Corps but never did we question Hanoi, Cambodia,

Or Saigon.

The seventies came and went as did the hippies and the flower

Children,

Though we were into jeans—for comfort—and long beards—

"To get back to our roots,"

Aghast if anyone thought we had learned from the hippies and the

Flower children.

Number threes took up with drugs, became frail shadows of their

Former selves;

Number twos married, divorced, remarried, and divorced again

And slept around to finally get through college and up the

Corporate ladder.

Number Ones we determined we had done right by:

They married after college, had two kids spaced two year

Apart-one of each sex—and joined granddad's old firm.

Miss Clairol, Grecian Formula, and jogging kept us young

But that poverty we'd planned to send our kids out to fight

Across the sea

Met us and LBJ at the front door.

Though we couldn't say we'd seen depression soup kitchens, we

Soon learned to run them, to hawk goods for charities, to

Volunteer to drive.

Our parents died; we became the older generation.

On integrity, we finally question Viet Nam,

Jane Fonda, and Richard Nixon;

Yet we never questioned our own ways.

We began to have inklings that somewhere back down the line

A bill of goods had come our way;

We'd bought it a piece at a time just like those Nazis and

Japanese of our preteen/teen years.

Our kids, too, were buying bills of "Elvis isn't dead," "AIDS

Is here to stay," "the education sys is all bad."

Is life always this way? Selling current bills of goods to

Those who listen to its vamping call?

Of is it choices or may even fate?

*8/20/89 8/29/98

MARY RETIRED

Only last year she moved up two flights. She climbed.

Dressed in correct black jacket, fashionably lapelled.

Dove gray blouse, black string tie, grey flannel

Skirt, grey house.

Low heeled black suide shoes, never patent.

Her possession: a black portfolio

Threading her way to her office

She spoke to a student, a faculty member, another student.

Once at her office door, she fished out keys,

Keys 'round a large metal circle, Dad-given.

She undid the lock; the door swung open.

On gray metal desk, she spread themes as

she worked with a student

Whose paper would not write itself.

Choose the right words himself,

His vocabulary being minuscule compared to hers.

Thirty years of this routine have past,

Slid by.

Today she is Mary,

Retired.

Revised 1998

MARY, RETIRED

Over the sands she moves slowly,

Dressed in peasant dress of stripes: beige

By the face, turquoise 'crossed the breast, sun

Yellow about the waist, green circle 'round

The hips, red flounce. Pink thongs. A red floppy

Brimmed hat, sometimes carried, sometimes held on

The back of her graying hair. A black Le Bag in hand.

Finding her spot, she spreads a green towel. She pats

it flat, turning a flipped corner aright.

On the towel, she arranges a red change

purse, two papayas, a paring knife,

A tall carafe of orange juice, Waverly crackers,

Nail crème,

Remover,

Cotton balls, sun tan

Lotion,

A slim volume of Ciardi's.

A beige canvas-backed

Slant seat.

Completing these preparations,

She turns to face a stopping

San Diego city bus.

From the bus emerge children: Holland, Michelle, Curtis.

"Momma-on-the-bus, what do you

have for us today?"

Fall 1984

SUSIE'S GRANDS

They were eight, all roses in her memory's garden patch:

The first a girl, dark, solemn. always thinking, a doll, a purse, a powder can.

The second a boy, fair, blonde, protective of his toys, a tattletale;

The third a girl blonde, curly hair, a true thumb sucker;

A boy the fourth, premature, a two finger sucker;

The fifth a blonde sturdy boy destined to play baseball and golf;

The sixth another boy, fragile, not long for this world but loved;

The seventh another blonde boy, golfer, dry wit;

And last a happy girl, a lover of family and her dog.

All her grandchildren, all loved, all precious in her sight.

October '03

LEAVES

In the early dawn, the cotton wood's leaves danced in the fall breeze,

Golden and green on stems of brown.

By noon the wind tore at them, whirling them about like toy pinwheels

Twisting this way and that until they tore from their branches and swept to
The ground.

By evening they lay in heaps along the roadway,

There to be crushed by homeward bound commuters.

October 29, '03

NATURE SONG

Wind song

Sand song

Gritty

Brown

Scoring tiled earth

Wind song

Rain song

Gummy

Oozing

Sticky earth.

THE CATTLE

The pasture's strewn with calves
Lying in piles, sleeping, soaking up
Sun and growth.

The white Brahmas graze, all heads south.
A whistle signals a freight.
The calves,
The cows look up to note
The engine as it comes.
They watch as though counting cars:
Grain, oil, chemicals.
The caboose appears; and as it moves
Along the track.
Heads turn slowly to follow it
Along the steely track.

For minutes they stare after
The vanishing caboose.
Then heads move downward.
Now all face north
To graze the other way.

April 12, '85

THE CHANGE

Last fall I stood

Looking over fields,

A patio view of

Dead grass,

Lean cattle.

Drought.

This spring waters came.

Now I stand in that self same spot

Viewing blue grass

Bag heavy cows

Fatted calves

Black-nosed calves

And zooming honey bees.

THE FARMER AND HIS DOG

The newborn sleeps alone

Its mom's primitive protection

Instincts still rising

Though long kine have been fenced,

Patched small,

Protected by farmer and his dog.

The farmer and dog come

The heifer turns,

Walks away down field.

She lows. The babe lies

Still; the farmer and his dog know the

Game.

She circles; they prowl the

Babe lies still, nose down,

Ears back to catch their sounds.

They spot the babe. And as

They move toward the babe;

The heifer dashes.

The babe jumps up, its legs planted

Straight, tense. It wheels.

The farmer misses as he grabs

For an ear, a leg. The

Dog gives chase.

Next time he sees this calf

He'll pen him,

Do the job civilization leads him

To perform to stay in keeping with

Its rules

Written while a colleague gave a presentation

April 12, '85

THE PLANE

I wonder if Orville and Wilbur

Envisioned such as this.

No, they saw man flying,

Riding high on thermal waves,

Enjoying flight as

Eagles seem to.

A MERE CRICK

On the ground they call it

"The Mighty Mississip"

But from my flight, way up,

I call it a crick, twining

'mong mosaic patches,

Varied brown-hued shapes

Which mark planting time for

Farmers 'long banks

In Arkansas and Louisian'.

May '85

A PHENOMENON

Dulles: a necessary stop to satisfy an agency.

Yet as we descend, an escort joins to

Accompany us to land.

It moves along across the land, trees, cows, and barns.

It moves closer as further down

We glide.

We two'll surely collide as closer still

We speed

Until at last we two are nearly one

Racing down the paved runway to pause at

Terminal.

At takeoff, the reverse occurs.

Then, we two part. He's gone. Lost.

We're up too far to cast a shadow on the Earth.

We're flying high, too high.

May '85

OKALHOMA

In late June, I like Oklahoma from high in the air.

Its blocks of land outlined by roads and fences,

Highways curling through pastures, through fields

And green forests,

Creeks and rivers sauntering toward sparking lakes,

Blocks of soil: browns, reds, beiges,

Grain waving green and gold,

Towns and homesteads, ranches,

Sprawling OKC, Goodwell rolling flat.

But on the ground, ticks and flies pester man and beast;

Humidity's high, high as the elephant's eye;

Storm clouds rise; tornadoes come; hail pounds the crops

Plumb flat,

Beasts wade out into ponds escaping the heat.

Okies—all hues of them—wave fans or quickly close doors

To houses great and small, closing in refrigerated air:

Most of the year I sing of Oklahoma and her waving fields of grain,

But in summer I only sing such praise when I'm up thirty thousand feet.

I sing of Oklahoma and her waving fields of grain;

But in summer, be sure I am observing her

From thirty thousand feet!

June 22'85

WHY

I'd like to know why

Air travel brings out in me

The urge to create

A poem, a rhyme, more doggerel than verse.

At no other time in my writing life

Can I create such words.

Is it the sky? The altitude?

Those airscape views

That make me grab a pen,

A scrap of paper to record

The things I see when

I lift off from Earth?

March 3 '86

WEATHER

We flew north from warm Oklahoma
Where hyacinths were in bloom
To cool Chicago where I expected snow.

But in Chicago, only Lake Michigan
And ponds lay frozen.
The streets, the parkways ran bare.
The sun shining; sky, clear.

A fifteen minute flight to Frankfort,
Just southeast, revealed snow covered
Fields bound by
Highways and homesteads black and clear.

Further southeast Columbus lay
Tucked in snow;
And further still low lying clouds
Hid Tennessee from view.
Washington we finally see
Traced lightly by the snow
The air, crisp; the sky, blue.

March 3 '86

CHICAGO

Chicago from 15,000 feet up

Is not Sandburg's at all.

No hog butcher. No.

It's orange-lined squares of houses.

It's swirls of clover leaves,

It's orange-edged border tracing

A Lake Erie water front.

There's a Southern garden pattern.

It's Shee Kah Go of the famous song

Mystic, romantic, bright

From 15 up.

It tugs the night owl's yen

To do the town up red.

No, it's not Sandburg's Chcago.

It's Shee Kah Go after dark,

A necklace of white light

One odd shaped spot

A line of car lights tracking a street

To a high night life.

June '86, September 7, '98

AA PLANES

American Airline planes have many things in common:

Silver bodies marked with reed and blue AA's
Sprouting wings.

Inside the aisles vary only in color.
On this flight reds and oranges;
On another blues, greys, and taupes.
The ruggy wall hangings are the same;
The seats so-so;
Color makes the only difference.

Attendants are much the same:
Crest smiles pleasant, accommodating,
Varying only by sex, hair color, age, race.
And the food's the same, flight after
Flight after flight:
Breakfast: pancake and OJ
Snack: corned beef, Swiss cheese, a Kaiser roll
Or peanuts and a coke.
Lunch: small lettuce salad, spicy meat,
An apple-nothing dessert
Dinner: more of lunch
Rearranged to fool the eyes.

THE SIGN

Breakfast. Vegetarian.

Nuts, raisins, fruit,

Whole wheat

While others ate

Sausages and omlets

Biscuits, jelly, yellow butter

Truly disappointed that

I had faked

An unusual interest

In diet keeping that day.

Disgruntled, I chewed raisins, nuts,

And coveted the others' meals.

I turned to the window

And looking west I saw

A perfect rainbow circle.

Encompassing a center circle,

Rainbowed as well.

On we flew;

The rainbow circle grew.

We should have passed it

But as we flew;

The clouds disappeared;

The rainbow circle faded

Into the snow patched earth.

And I felt almost cleansed:

I'd stuck to my diet

And I could see

A weight loss in the end.

January '87

UNCROSSED PATHS

I'D NEVER SEEN THIS BEFORE.

Three jet streams paralleled beneath our plane,

Marking where one had been.

Where had it come from?

Where had it gone?

I fathomed neither.

But as I sit, grazing out on its path

I breathe a grateful prayer.

The planes had not crossed paths:

His a bit higher;

Ours a bit lower;

His a bit later;

Ours a bit sooner, or

It would have been else.

March 9, '86

AN ALPINE VILLAGE

From my vantage point

The town was an Alpine village

'Neath a Christmas tree:

Each house lighted at each window.

Reflections spilling over

To winter's white rain

Firs by doorways neat;

Smoke curling from chimneys,

Free of winter's white rain

That stretches to lake hard by,

To hills rising just beyond.

It is all there.

Only this is Ohio

After January's blizzard

January '86

REPLICATION

Above, the clouds replicated the snow covered earth.

Mountains rose; valleys dipped;

Road-like tracks stretched out

Across the undulating fields.

Missing from the cloudscape

Were the townships square, oblong, odd-shaped;

Missing were patches made by man's roadways and paths.

Missing were the rumblings of truck, the low of cows, the babblings of men.

Here only God abode in a pristine world of white,

A pristine world of quiet

UNDONE

I.

I've had it.

I may never fly again.

American's name is tarnished forevermore

If things don't change.

Tarmac sitting is not my

Game. Neither is switching me.

Nor can I abide plane breakdowns though

I'm glad we weren't winging

When it occurred.

What I'd like is punctuality

On AA's part as well as

Mine. And certainly security

When I fly the friendly skies.

It's the airline that's unfriendly!

2

Today I forgot to read

My Bible before I left.

I didn't even pray God my

Substitute to help.

Instead I went about to play,

To gaze on shops and

To eat with friends from states afar.

And gab the whole day through.

Perhaps the lack of sought for

Blessing made

God think today that

Since I vacationed from His Word and Him

That He vacationing would do.

For here I sit in winged craft

Hoping for take off two hours late

Enroute home a different way

Because my scheduled flight

Fell through.

3

Washington skyline!

Who wants to see you now?

Your jets coming in to land over Potomac gray

Your domed capitol building

Gleaming in dying sun,

A yellow-lined black tarmac parallel

As Washington Monument pierces skies of blue

Right now I'd prefer to see

The checkered lands of Indiana

With soils of varied brownish hues

The evergreens of Illinois

The tarmac of O'Hare.

I want to be on my way home!

MEDITATION

I spent the day in idle meditation

On ephemeral icebergs on blue seas.

Here sails a ship gargantuan,

It's upper deck so high that even though phantom passengers wave

I see not their adieus.

An iceberg floats, its edges ragged but untearing

Below three wisps align themselves

By docks miraged.

Unbaked meringue puffs punctuate the blue

White alps appear,

Some low, some tower.

Between the roads, mosaic patches wander

Beyond a monstrous range has plateaus high

Such 'scapes entertain as one sits out

A cross country flight.

PATCHES

Patches lie

    Beneath us"

Patches of pecan S

             A

                N

                 D

    Chocolate

       a bl d.

      M r e

Patches of   p   n

      I l   e   I t

    T   e   r   e   o

  s   d g n p   s.

Patches   by f   de

   Variegated   a   cid

               L   u

          L's   ous blossoms.

      Colonials

  Ling

  Veal

  Re.

Spr   ing   ran
Ng   awl   ches.
Ri
Ba

small   distinguish   sky.
Sing   clusters   able   the
Clo   un   from

ALL GONE;

Nothing now but masses. Not patches but masses of bumpy white.

Not patches but

Darkening white

Masses, throwing

Red jaggers around our

Slender

Sliver

Ar

Ro

w.

HOSTAGE

The airline captures you

Holds you hostage

Until Armistice Day.

F	f	t	then,
I	l	h	you
R	l	e	queue
S	e		up
T	r	s	each flying
		K	time,
Y	s	y	foot shifting,
O	u		bags shuffled up,
u	l	i	until they join others
	L	f	moving up to board more
s	i		quickly than you ever can
I	n	y	
G	g	o	you arrive at Gate 0 to
N		u	stand in line while
	Y		babies and old ladies
O	o	b	and first class saunter on,
N	u	u	oblivious of the queue.
	R	t	

A　　　　　　　　a　　d　　y　　m　　!

S　m　f　　　　t　　e　　o　　a
　　l　l　　　　s　　u　　d　　Five jets
　　　　　　　　　　　　　　　　idle

A　l　y　　　　f　　t　　　　e　　by at
　　　　　　　　　　　　　　　　different

N　e　　　　　　i　　i　　t　　　　heights;
　　　　　　　　　　　　　　　　the

　　S　x　　　　n　　n　　h　　i　　airport
　　　　　　　　　　　　　　　　sits be-

A　　　　　　　a　　a　　i　　t　　low.
　　　　　　　　　　　　　　　　You six

D　f　m　　　　l　　t　　n　　　　bank
　　　　　　　　　　　　　　　　right

v　o　i　　　　　　i　　k　　b　　together
　　　　　　　　　　　　　　　　to come

A　r　l　　　　　　o　　　　u　　around
　　　　　　　　　　　　　　　　one
　　　　　　　　　　　　　　　　more

N　　　l　　　　　　n　　y　　t　　time at
　　　　　　　　　　　　　　　　least.

T　p　i　　　　　　　　o

A　l　ol　　　　　　　u　　n

G　e　n　　　　　　　'　　o

e　　　　　　　　　　v

　　l　m　　　　　　　e

98

N   i

l

e

s.

t   The pilot guides the plane to ground below

o   As   you roll to queue again, the

          three   fifth of the six planes

Q   pilots   taxiing for miles to assign-

U   just   ed gate.

E   parallel   you

U   to   queue

E   you   again

          Queue   behind

A   again   suave yuppies

G   as   hunched grannies

A   jaunty   and

I   piper   leftover hippies.

n.   cubs

         zoom   In the queue, march to baggage

         down   only to break into

         the   shorter queues to seize

         runway   bags before they pass

         to   another.

become	Queue
airborn	at long
seconds	term parking
before	pass through
the	toll line,
tarmac	diesel
ends.	Perfumed.

F   the family queues

I   to plant welcoming

N   kisses as you

A   declare: "Home, home

L   at last."

L

y.

GOD

God is my crying post.

God is my physician.

God is my counselor.

God is my advocate.

God is my caretaker.

God is my light.

God is my champion.

God is my benefactor.

God is my provider.

God is my support.

God is my all in all.

EVOLVER?

If I evolved I want to meet
The force behind evolving me.
I want to meet the one who makes
This body of mine do all the things
It does so automatically.

The hair to grow., the nails, too,
The blood pulsate, the digestion churn,
The urge to love, the urge to eat,
The overwhelming urge to sleep
E'vn while blood flows, heart beats
And the digestive mechanism works.

Say, you, who insist that I
Evolved from a micro-organism from the sea,
Say, where's the one who organized me
And set these functions into BE?

September '88

TIMES

Neaderthal man plodded

But God

God walked

God walked out

God walked out on

God walked out on space.

And on God's space out walked

Edward White

Dave Irwin

Neal Armstrong

Eugene Cernan

October '79

HIS CROWN

His crown was only thorns;

The Romans thought it fine.

In truth it was, for

As he hung there on the cross

It pierced His brow so fair.

Some thorns were for those

Who listened but did not hear.

Some thorns were for those Romans

Standing by Him there.

Others were for generations to come,

Our forefathers, if you will.

One was for me; it pierced Him deep

My sins so many are.

Yet willingly He wore those thorns

That I might live again.

Alas, alas, one was for me;

That one pierced him deep,

For my sins piled high as

Nebo's crowning peak.

One would think He'd scorn me

For piercing Him so

But willingly went He to wear

That piercing crown

That I might live again.

Thorns! Thorns!

That's all His crown was made of

Say men who know Him not.

But the man who knows Him humbly says,

"Those thorns were sins of mine."

1991

THE DEBT

The Son of Man gave His life for us

What a price for a handful of dust!

Yet He thought us worthy

Worthy through His blood.

How can we repay this debt,

This debt of love we owe?

Give to Him our all, yes, all,

And live out love to honor Him.

November '87

GOD CLEANED HIS WORLD

God cleaned His world this morning:

He scrubbed the maple green

And bathed the mistletoe

Sponged the pansies' faces

And washed the roses' petals

Rinsed the grasses down.

Drip-dried the hibiscus blossoms

And spot cleaned the anemones

Then patted dry the leaves and flowers

With his automated wind machine

SUNDAY

It is Sunday
And God smiles
As worshipers move toward church.

Singing His praises,
Calling Him Father, Savior, Guide,
Prince of Peace, Wonderful, Master.

Praying to Him, praising Him,
Confessing sins both hidden and open,
Asking for bread and thanking Him.

Listening to His called one
As His message comes to them.
Heeding the message,
Coming to confess and rededicate
And bring the lost to Him.

God smiles
And agrees with His Son.
The sacrifice at Calvary was
Worth it all.

Fall '87

ON WAKING

I awake, O Lord, to find
That You have given us a
Perfect day to live.
Help us to use it well
So we can say in morning hence:

Yesterday was a day
To cherish for a life time.
I lived it for God;
I enjoyed it as
His gift to me
To use as though
It were my only one.

December 1990

A MODEL

I chose a model

An older teen named Jim.

He was tough, a fighter.

H sneaked in dirty words.

He puffed; he drank;

He made light of good.

Then I chose as model

Elvis and his dress

His shoes, tight pants,

His swagger, his hair

His twist, his blue

Suede shoes.

At twenty-five, I looked about

I finally saw the real man.

He'd been there all the time.

Dear Dad, steady, good and kind.

He'd kept me on his heart

'Til finally I saw

He was the greatest model

A boy could ever have.

Now to you, my grandson,

I say:

Be careful, little man

Whom you choose to model.

He can lead down

Paths that lead

To images and places

Where no man ought to go.

Choose the greatest model

A boy can ever have:

Your dad who's steady, good and kind.

He holds you in his heart.

September '95; September '98

PRAYER

Oh, our Father

This we pray:

Keep us to be back

Next season to worship You.

Help us, Lord, to worship You

Throughout this year,

To lean on You

To see Your face

To do Your bidding

All the time

Until You bring us

To this season once again

To worship and adore

Your Blessed Son Immanuel

Amen.

December 2000

THE COMMAND

God asked me to take a stand:

I flinched and sought escape.

I turned to Him and said.

"Remember You had Jeremiah write,

"I will put my law in their minds

And write it on their hearts'?

"I've done that, God;

Isn't that enough?"

He looked at me; He shook His head.

He said in tones so kind,

"My child, I am in your heart.

You did obey by taking responsibility

For your own sins. That's good;

But, my child, I sent My Son

And He says to you as He did to the

Eleven others as Matthew does record.

Not only were you to accept Him

You were to take your stand

By being baptized to show the world

That you are Mine.

"Truly you are Mine;

But I want you to tell the world,

I'm God's."

"I tell, you world, I'm God's."

June 24, 1990

RESURRECTED

Women came to the tomb

So early that first day.

They found the tomb empty,

Bereft of God's own Son.

Running, they bore the message.

Horrors! The Master is gone.

John and Peter came running;

John stopped without

To marvel that the stone was moved.

Peter dashed in to see

If

The Master were really gone.

John stepped in and spied the clothes

Lying undisturbed but empty.

He believed! He believed!

Returning home they wondered

Where He had gone

But Mary stayed a-weeping

A-weeping for her Lord.

Two angels came to tell her

"He is not here—look, not here.

He's risen as He said

He is the Risen Lord."

Mary turned still weeping

She did not understand.

Questioned she another;

The gardener she thought.

"Where have you taken my Jesus?"

She questioned as she wept.

Though He had spoken "Mary,"

She recognized not His voice.

Again He spoke; He called her name,

Her own, her personal name,

She recognized her Lord

Risen from the grave.

He was not gone; no one had stolen

His body without leave.

No one had concealed Him;

Nothing had contained Him.

He had risen from the dead! He rose that day to keep

The promise He had made

To rebuild the temple in three

Short days. New Testament prophecy

Fulfilled.

The Pharisees, the Sadducees lost

The fight they fought

Not knowing they had been used

By the God they thought they worshiped

To bring about the triumph

He had planned since Eden's fall.

They brought about the resurrection

Affirming Jesus' word

That He would go but would return

To carry believers to be with God

Forever and ever. Forever!

Resurrected! Resurrected!

To be with God

'Ever more

THE DREAM

I dreamed last night I was in Heaven

And there I interceded for my son.

"Oh, God," I said as I watched that adult son

Give too little change to a customer

And then pocket the excess,

"Forgive, my son, he needs more than his employer pays."

Then I saw son driving 45 in a zone marked

25 and pleaded,

"God, forgive him, for he is rushing home

To be with wife and my grand babes."

God looked at me with eyes so sad

And said calmly yet clearly,

"Dear one, you love your son as I loved Mine.

What has your son done for Mine?"

I stammered and I stuttered,

"Well, God, he gets to worship services

Twice a year

And every Sunday lets his wife and children go to church.

He bows his head when prayers are said

In his house or another's.

Surely, God, that's quite enough for such a loving boy

Who always honors his mom on her birthday

And your Son's.

He's only human, God,

You know, you made him human."

God looked at me again and said,

"Yes,

I made him human so he could think and choose

And he has chosen thusly.

My Son, what did He do for you and for your son?"

I gulped, "He died to give us life above."

I woke, fell to my knees and begged

My Lord's forgiveness

For thinking my son merited favors special

When God had given His

So mine could have life eternal.

May '03, February '05

JESUS/JUDAS

Judas' feelings mirrored
Men's feelings about Him;
Jesus, God's feelings about
Men.

One ran away, finding his end
In endless death;
The other stood, was vilified,
And rose to give
Endless life to all men
Who would believe in Him.

They stood beside each other
In the lanes of Galilee.
They stood beside each other
In all the regions round.
Yet they stood words apart
Judas and Jesus:
The one sold out his master;
The other obeyed His.
One stood with I
The focus of his eyes;
The other stood
His focus on us,
The to be apples of His eyes.

FARSIGHTED

I knew You said

"Jerusalem And Judea, too, but God

I thought those fields were for

Kids, old ladies, and pastors.

I always aimed

"For the uttermost parts of the earth."

God, we youth are strong

We can go where kids can't be sent,

Where old ladies can't make it 'cause of

Heat and flies and language barriers,

Where pastors have no time to go 'cause

Homefolk need them to marry, to comfort,

And to bury.

Today my mission field

Is right here where I am.

The haves of the world are here on my block;

The have=nots in the next; yet both have need of the message

You taught in Galilee.

"I am the Light of the world . . ..

No man cometh to the Father but by me."

They need to know those words—

I know those words.

God, you mean my mission field begins right here

Where people see me now?

Yes, God, You may lead me to "the uttermost

Parts of the world" next week or next year;

But today my field is here.

August '90